Organization
Development

Organization Development

**behavioral science interventions
for organization improvement**

WENDELL L. FRENCH
CECIL H. BELL, JR.

University of Washington

PRENTICE-HALL, INC., *Englewood Cliffs, New Jersey*

Library of Congress Cataloging in Publication Data

FRENCH, WENDELL L   1923–
  Organization development.

  Bibliography: p.
  1. Management.   2. Organizational change.
I. Bell, Cecil, 1935–   joint author. II. Title.
HD38.F69   658.4'06   72-2891
ISBN 0-13-641662-4
ISBN 0-13-641654-3 (pbk.)

Printed in the United States of America

10 9 8 7 6 5 4 3 2 1

Prentice-Hall International, Inc., London
Prentice-Hall of Australia, Pty. Ltd., Sydney
Prentice-Hall of Canada, Ltd., Toronto
Prentice-Hall of India Private Limited, New Delhi
Prentice-Hall of Japan, Inc., Tokyo

to

Marjorie and Dianne

Contents

Preface

This book is about an exciting and profound idea and about the growing body of knowledge related to that idea. The idea is this: it is possible for the people within an organization collaboratively to manage the culture of that organization in such a way that the goals and purposes of the organization are attained at the same time that human values of individuals within the organization are furthered.

The key to the subject to which this book is addressed, organization development, is contained in the phrase "collaborative management of the organization's culture." To *collaborate* is to labor together, as the derivation of the word suggests. To *manage* is to direct and control; to be in command of. *Organization culture* is the prevailing background fabric of prescriptions and proscriptions for behavior, the systems of beliefs and values, and the technology and task of the organization together with the accepted approaches to these. An organization's culture serves powerfully as a determinant of behavior. If the culture supports behaviors appropriate for organization goal attainment, the result will probably be an effective organization; if the culture supports behaviors obviating goal attainment, the result will probably be an ineffective organization.

In addition, the organization's culture may operate to enhance human values or may operate to thwart them. By human values we mean those goals and strivings of individuals that relate to what they want from the organization and from their participation as organization members. Some human values that seem to be important today are the following: the opportunity to make a meaningful contribution to the organization; the opportunity to have satisfying interpersonal relationships; the opportunity to accept responsibility; the opportunities for recognition and advancement; the opportunities to stretch oneself and to grow.

An overriding human value that is gaining ascendance is the belief that the individual has worth and value and should be treated accordingly. All too frequently, however, this value is given less than adequate attention, either from lack of knowledge about how to implement this value in ways congruent with the furtherance of organizational goals or from adherence to a fallacious dilemma, or both. In this regard we eschew the fallacy that *either* the organization *or* the individual must be deprived of its objectives for the service of the other. (The issue is popularly stated as a faulty dilemma as follows: In the satisfaction of goals and objectives, must the organization give in to the individual or must the individual give in to the organization? Stating the issue in this way implies that there are no other alternatives, for example, that both can satisfy their goals simultaneously. Or, perhaps, that neither can.)

We believe that organization development offers today's best answer to the interdependent problems of improving organizations and enhancing individual worth. The focus of organization development is the total organization, but, as we shall see, not to the disservice of the individual.

Most of us are aware that there are both "formal" and "informal" domains in organizational culture—that there is a network of formalized elements such as policies, rules, procedures, equipment, hierarchy of authority, and the like, and that there is also an informal "underground" of feelings, attitudes, and behaviors that is much less visible but nevertheless exists and has a major impact on organizational outcomes. Organization development is an open strategy for increasing the congruence between these two domains and at the same time releasing a great deal of energy that can be used for creativity and cooperation. The essence of the OD process is for organizational members to help describe the culture of the organization, to help plan what it should be like in an ideal sense, and to assist in getting the organization from what it is to what it should be.

Organization development is the name given to the emerging applied behavioral science discipline that seeks to improve organizations through planned, systematic, long-range efforts focused on the organization's culture and its human and social processes. The goals of organization development are to make the organization more effective, more viable, and better able to achieve both the goals of the organization as an entity and the goals of the individuals within the organization. As a discipline, OD develops and implements theories, technology, and researches directed toward improving total systems—a different task from that of developing individual managers. The means of OD are behavioral science and structural interventions into the ongoing organization. These interventions may focus on culture, processes, and events at many levels of the organization, ranging from individuals, and pairs and trios, to small groups, two or more groups, and the total organization. In the interventions there is an emphasis on interpersonal, group, and intergroup behaviors and dynamics, but this emphasis is not exclusive, for changes in job design and changes in the organization's structure may result from or be a part of OD efforts.

OD, with its focus on developing total organizations, represents a new thrust in management practice. Furthermore, the rapidly expanding technology of OD has made available some powerful and efficacious tools for improving total systems. OD programs may be found in many countries and in many different kinds of organizations. It is probable that organization development will be around for a long time and will increasingly be a methodology chosen for effecting organizational change and improvement.

In this book we present what we think is the field of organization development: we show where it came from and where it may be going, and we give the reader a look at both the theory and the practice of OD. We have attempted to include most of what is known about OD at the current time—the state-of-the-art. In this way we have included a blend of material that we hope will make the work relevant to academicians, to students who may want to study OD, to OD specialists, and to practicing managers who may want to try to improve their organizations.

In this book we have generally attempted to describe organization development as we think it should be conducted, that is, by successful applications of OD efforts. This is not intended to suggest that all OD programs are successful or faultless, for they are not. We do analyze pitfalls and problems that can arise in practice, and we discuss a number of the value and contingency dilemmas inherent in the field.

We would like to say a few words about stability. Although this is a book about change—to develop or to improve an organization is to change it—we want to assert that in our opinion stability and relative permanence have worth in organizations too. Worship at the altar of Change has become quite stylish, but in its advocacy few ask, Change for what purposes? What should we *not* change? We believe that much in the life, culture, and dynamics of organizations can be improved and should be changed; many things need not be changed. Organizational development means examining organizational culture and keeping the good things, modifying some, and eliminating others. It is not a cutting loose from tested values and assumptions, but it does involve a searching look to see which practices and norms are functional and which are not. Many features or phenomena about organizations have contributed to their growth, relevance, adaptiveness, responsiveness; these should be identified and kept.

There is stability in the organization development process itself. The scientific method, which is inherent in OD efforts, is basically an orderly process of inquiry, data gathering, and testing of hypotheses. OD is not erratic, random, and precipitous. It is systematic and methodical, and above all, human.

We have been influenced by the writings and work of many people, many of whom are cited in the chapters that follow. We are particularly indebted to the pioneering work of Chris Argyris, Richard Beckhard, Kenneth Benne, Warren Bennis, Robert Blake, Leland Bradford, Robert Chin, Sheldon Davis, Rensis Likert, Ronald Lippitt, Floyd Mann, Douglas McGregor, Jane Mouton, and Herbert Shepard. Special help was provided by Robert Blake, Ronald Lippitt, and Herbert Shepard, who corresponded with us about the history of OD and reacted to that emerging chapter. Anthony Raia read the entire manuscript and provided valuable suggestions and feedback. We also want to acknowledge our indebtedness to our clients and coconsultants, from whom we have learned a great deal. The secretarial staff of our own Management and Organization Department was very helpful in the preparation of the manuscript; we particularly wish to thank Nona Pedersen and Sandra Goodman for their excellent help.

Wendell French
Cecil Bell

1

An Introduction to Organization Development

illustrations

definition

history

1

Some Illustrations of Organization
Development Efforts

This is a book about organization development—a planned, systematic process in which applied behavioral science principles and practices are introduced into an ongoing organization toward the goals of effecting organization improvement, greater organizational competence, and greater organizational effectiveness. The focus is on organizations and their improvement, or to put it another way, the focus is on *total system change.* The orientation is on action—achieving desired results as a consequence of planful activities. The setting is real organizations in the real world.

In this book we tell the broad story of organization development (OD); we examine the nature, history, assumptions, strategies and models, intervention activities, and ramifications of organization development. To begin, let us look at some examples of what might happen in an organization as a result of instituting OD efforts. Although the settings of the following illustrations are in business firms, a public school, and an American Indian tribe, the settings and organizations could be any of a wide range of organizations. Labor unions, volunteer organizations, industrial plants, governmental units, service organizations, small and multinational corporations, research and development laboratories—all of these offer appropriate settings for organization development programs. The key, of course, is that where there is an organization that seeks improvement, there is the opportunity for an OD effort.

ILLUSTRATION 1: PROBLEMS IN A BUSINESS FIRM

Problems of lack of cooperation between subunits, increasing complaints from customers, sagging morale, and rapidly increasing costs induced the president of a medium-sized company to confer with a

3

behavioral scientist consultant about ways to improve the situation. The two talked at length, and it became apparent to the consultant that the executive, while having some apprehensions, was generally agreeable to the desirability of examining the dynamics of the situation, including decision-making processes and his own behavior. He and the consultant agreed that certain organization development efforts might be worthwhile. It was decided that a three-day workshop away from the usual routine, with the executive and his entire work team, might be an appropriate way to start.

The president then sounded out several of his subordinates about the possibility of the workshop, and reactions ranged from enthusiasm to some uneasiness. It was agreed to have the consultant meet with the executive and all his immediate subordinates to explain the typical format of such a meeting and to discuss the probable content of such a workshop. At the end of this meeting, the group decided to give it a try.

A few days before the off-site session, the consultant spent an hour interviewing each member of the team. In essence he asked them, What things are getting in the way of this unit being as successful as you would like it to be? The purpose of these interviews was to obtain the data around which the design of the workshop was to be built.

At the beginning of the workshop, the consultant first reported back to the group the general themes in the interviews which he had grouped under these problem headings: "The Boss," "Meetings," "Administrative Services," "Customer Relations," "Relations between Departments," and "Long-Range Goals." The group then prioritized these problem themes in terms of importance and immediacy and chose the problem areas to be worked on. With the consultant acting more as a coach than as a moderator, the group then examined the underlying dynamics of each problem area and examined optional solutions to problems. In addition to making suggestions for breaking into subgroups to tackle certain agenda items, and in addition to providing several ten-minute lecturettes on such topics as decision making and team effectiveness, the consultant intervened from time to time to comment on the way the group was working together and to help make explicit the norms under which the group seemed to be operating.

The last morning was spent developing "next action steps" relative to a dozen or so items discussed under the above headings. One of the decisions was to spend a half day with the consultant three months in the future for the purpose of reviewing progress toward problem solutions.

During a subsequent meeting between the company president and the consultant, the executive reported that the morale of the group was up substantially and customer complaints and costs were beginning to go down but that "we still have a long way to go, including making our staff meetings more effective." The two then agreed to have the consultant sit in on two or three staff meetings prior to the three-month review session.

The three-month review session with the consultant revealed that significant progress had been made on some action steps but that improvement seemed to be bogged down, particularly in areas requiring delegation of certain functions by the president to his key subordinates. This matter was extensively worked on by the group, and the president began to see where and how he could "loosen the reins," thus freeing himself for more long-range planning and for more contacts with key customers.

During the following years, the top management team institutionalized an annual three-day "problem-solving workshop" involving the consultant. In addition, each of the top managers utilized the consultant's services in conducting comparable workshops with their own subordinates. Over this period, the consultant and the personnel director, whose hiring had been a direct outgrowth of one of the sessions, began to work as a consulting team to the organization, with the personnel director gradually assuming more and more of the role of a "change agent." In addition to having planning and control responsibilities in the areas of employment and compensation and in other traditional personnel functions, the new personnel director also coordinated a management development program designed to supplement the company's problem-solving workshops. For example, managers were supported in their requests to attend specialized seminars in such areas as budgeting and finance, group dynamics, and long-range planning. The personnel director thus assumed an expanded role in which he served as an internal OD consultant to the operating divisions, as a linking pin with the external (original) consultant, and as a coordinator of the traditional personnel functions.

ILLUSTRATION 2: START-UP OF A NEW JUNIOR HIGH SCHOOL

A school district in a suburb outside a middle-size city had just finished building its third junior high school. The new principal was a young man, well known and liked in the district. He and two vice-principals selected the faculty (about thirty persons) and the adjunct staff—librarian, cooks, and custodians. With approval from the school district, the principal contacted the regional office of the NTL–Institute for Applied Behavioral Science and requested a one-week human relations laboratory for the new school faculty and staff. The NTL–Institute office referred the principal to one of its network members, and the week's activities were set up between the consultant and the principal.

It was apparent to the consultant that this situation represented a typical "start-up" situation in which a group of relative strangers were being called upon to form themselves into an interdependent team in order to accomplish some organizational mission. Typical issues in this kind of situation are the following: getting acquainted, learning about each other's expressive and communicative styles, clarifying roles, achieving identification with and acceptance of organization goals, determining how each member's activities fit into and contribute to organizational goals, and exploring the nature of the demands of the interdependencies of the organization members.

The week's activities were designed to address these issues. Starting with some get-acquainted activities, the group then turned its attention to exploring the nature of interpersonal communications, improving interpersonal communications skills, and exploring issues of trust, openness, and concern for each other. Next, attention was given to determining what kind of organization the members wanted to build together, what kind of climate they wanted to have, and how they could build themselves into an effective team. The thrust of this latter set of activities related to the school's organization structure and processes, to an understanding of organization dynamics and behavior, and then to building collaboratively the organization structure and processes that the members thought would both allow them to achieve organizational goals and allow them to enhance their individual goals. This included looking at the kind of leadership style and behavior they wanted from the principal and the two assistant principals, and it also included an expression of the desires and expectations of the administrators. Considerable attention was given to what Schein calls the "psychological contract"—the set of expectations the organization members have toward the organization and its hierarchical representatives regarding influence and control, and the set of expectations the organization has toward the members regarding performance and commitment.[1] The group also examined how they wanted to solve problems and make decisions as a team as they resolved problems common to their task accomplishment. A particularly important theme during the week was how the group was going to make decisions as a group. At the end of what seemed to be a successful week, they indicated that they had grown much closer together, that they valued the individual differences and contributions of the various members, and that they knew how to attack and solve the upcoming task problems of the new year. In addition, they had developed skills enabling them to look at their own processes (the way they got things done). So two major themes identified the week's activities: (1) developing better interpersonal rela-

[1] Edgar H. Schein, *Organizational Psychology* (Englewood Cliffs, N.J.: Prentice-Hall, Inc., 1965), pp. 10–11.

tions and interpersonal skills and (2) building the skills necessary to achieve and maintain an effective organization.

After the week was over, the consultant suggested to the principal that the members of school staff continue to work at their own organization development through periodically looking at how well they were achieving the goals and procedures that they had established and through taking "refresher" courses in these matters. To this end, three in-service training days (days in which the teachers furthered their professional development) were given over to refresher courses in which the total school staff as a "family group" looked inward at itself and its processes.

The following summer a second one-week laboratory was held with the same participants and the same consultant. There were several focuses: first, the group examined its successes and failures of the past school year in an attempt to learn how to improve its functioning. Second, the group devoted attention to developing the knowledge and skills necessary to generate its own valid data about the organization—its climate, culture, organization dynamics and processes—in order to manage these better. Again, during the second summer workshop, group members worked on problems relevant to their real world work problems; again the entire staff and faculty were in attendance; again they worked on interpersonal relations, as these were instrumental in building the organization that they wanted. The second summer was spent almost entirely on understanding organization dynamics and on ways of generating and utilizing valid information about the organization climate and culture. In-service training days following the second summer were again given over to the organization development activities.

Reactions to the program were favorable. Participants subsequently reported that they worked together well and that they enjoyed the climate of the school. They are currently convinced that they are doing a high quality job of teaching and educating. They call the summer workshops "hard work, but worth it," and they trace organization procedures to the learnings of the workshops. The school is viewed in the district as a model school and a desirable place to get transferred to. The school has experienced low turnover of staff and faculty.

ILLUSTRATION 3: DEPARTURE FROM TRADITION IN A DIVISION OF A LARGE CORPORATION

Stemming initially from the enthusiasm of the labor relations director and a member of the board, some efforts had been made by a few key executives of a large multidivision company to apply emerging behavioral science ideas to the solution of problems being faced by the corporation. In one division, the top manager and his staff experimented, successfully they felt, with team-building sessions augmented by workshops on leadership style and decision making. In the team-building sessions intact work groups looked at their tasks and at their ways of working, and they attempted to clarify the roles and responsibilities necessary for better task accomplishment. The sessions typically revolved around finding answers to the question, How can we build ourselves into a more effective team? The process was being continued at successively lower levels in the organization. In a second division, a major "job enrichment" program was being undertaken which had the immediate consequence of forcing a searching look at the prevailing leadership styles, the structure of the division, and the goals and roles of individuals within the division.

In another division, the top management team became interested in the use of attitude surveys and requested the help of a consultant through corporate headquarters. The consultant urged that there be extensive participation in the design of an attitude questionnaire, that the data be reported back to all who would participate, and that workshop settings be used. The workshop feature, in particular, was a departure from what the managers thought was traditional business practice, and there was some resistance to the idea because of fears of criticism. This was partially alleviated by a suggestion by the consultant to report the data in such a way as to minimize embarrassment to individual managers, and the management group agreed to go ahead with the questionnaire-plus-workshop approach.

The questionnaire included several items in the following categories: "Organizational Climate," "Pay and Benefits," "Relations with Other Units," "Communications," "Supervisor/Employee Relations," "My Job," and "Opportunities for Personal Growth and Advancement." Subsequently, responses to all items were tabulated for the total division as well as unit by unit. The division summary was reported to all units, but each specific unit tabulation was reported only to the unit involved to avoid misleading and perhaps destructive comparisons.

A team of consultants then worked with all the managers in the organization to design workshops for each unit. During these workshops the data were discussed as well as the probable forces giving rise to the various responses. Emphasis was on "How satisfied are we with the questionnaire responses?" and "What do we wish to improve?" rather than on any external criteria of performance. Action planning, which frequently included recommendations to higher management, was emphasized during the last part of each workshop.

While the workshops had their tense moments and were sometimes heavy going, reactions were generally quite positive. Typically, the manager, the consultants, and the participants agreed afterward that the meetings had been highly successful, that the process should continue throughout the division, and that the questionnaire and the workshops should be repeated in a year or two.

ILLUSTRATION 4: ORGANIZATIONAL IMPROVEMENT IN AN INDIAN TRIBE

A request to a graduate school of business from the tribal council and the executive director of an American Indian tribe for a management development workshop resulted in a counterproposal by a professor who had been approached for his reactions. The professor, who was also an organization development consultant, suggested, with the concurrence and support of a colleague, that the two faculty members visit the reservation, interview the key people in the tribal organization, and develop a workshop around the problems being experienced by the organization. This particular tribal organization was charged with responsibilities for the management of the natural resources of the reservation, for maintenance and development of utilities and services, for welfare and health, for law and order, for economic development, for management of tribal enterprises, and for preservation of the best of the tribal culture. The tribal organization was the governing body of the tribal members.

With the support of the chairman of the five-man tribal council, the council, and the executive director, it was agreed that a group of approximately twenty key people would be invited to the workshop as proposed by the consultants. These people included the total council, the executive director, his key subordinates, the staff of the Community Action Program, the Bureau of Indian Affairs resident forester, and an educator in charge of vocational education in the high school located on the reservation. All these people were interviewed by the consultants and were asked, in effect, What things are going right, and what things in the organization are getting in the way of accomplishing objectives? The two consultants extracted the central positive and negative themes from the interview data. These themes became the basic issues or problems around which the workshop was designed.

The first workshop, spanning an entire week, was held on the university campus and had two basic components which were intermixed throughout the week: (1) a continuation of the use of the *action research model* and (2) a lecture-exercise component. The action research model provided the basic flow of the workshop strategy as follows: data gathering (the preworkshop interviews plus additional data gathering during the workshop), data feedback, prioritizing of the problems, work on the problems, and action planning to solve the problems. This working of the problems that had been identified by the group served as the backdrop for the week's activities.

Several different types of interventions were initiated by the consultants during the problem-working phases of the workshop. Early in the workshop they presented the *force-field-analysis* technique to the participants, who were then asked to use the diagnostic tool in analyzing several of the issues the group had identified as high priority items. At another point, a modified *role analysis* technique was used relative to the roles of councilmen and executive director. With the council listening, the other participants discussed the following topic printed on a large sheet of newsprint: "If the council members were operating in an optimally effective and efficient way, what would they be doing?" Responses about which there seemed to be substantial consensus were made visible on the large sheet taped on the wall. Council members then were encouraged to respond, and subsequent discussion resulted in some modifications on the sheets. The exercise was then repeated for the executive director's role. With the executive director listening, the rest of the group discussed the question: "If the executive director were operating in an optimally effective and efficient way, what would he be doing?" One of the outcomes of this exercise was a gradual, but significant, shift in delegation of day-to-day operating decisions from the council to the executive director and staff.

The workshop also included several short lectures on a number of relevant topics including leadership, group process, decision making, problem diagnosis, and communications. This component also included some instrumented exercises that permitted participants to compare different decision-making models and to evaluate their usefulness.

By the end of the workshop, the participants had worked through a dozen or so important problems or issues and had agreed on next action steps, that is, "who was going to do what when." Results of a questionnaire administered on the last day of the workshop indicated overwhelming enthusiasm for the process and what had been accomplished. The consultants also perceived what they thought was a substantially higher level of openness, trust, and support between the participants at the end of the workshop compared with what was evident during the early part of the workshop.

One of the action steps that was agreed upon was a two-day follow-up visit to the reservation by the consultants to occur in five or six months. During ensuing weeks it became apparent that a follow-up visit sooner than that would be beneficial. The implementation of some action plans had bogged down, although important progress had been made on a number of others.

During the first follow-up visit the consultants interviewed a cross-section of the workshop participants to assess the degree of progress, met with the council to assist in a further review of council activities, and assisted in correcting a misunderstanding as to who was to be on one of the task forces created at the workshop. During the second follow-up visit the time of the consultants was primarily devoted to meetings with the executive director and the council members, although some discussions with key supervisors also occurred.

Subsequently, the council and the executive director requested a second workshop, with the suggestion that this workshop be shorter and that more time be devoted to follow-up on the reservation. The workshop was held at a resort; it started on a Tuesday evening and ended Friday afternoon.

Although the same basic pattern was followed for the second workshop, including preworkshop interviews, less time was spent on lectures and instrumented exercises and almost all the time was spent on substantive issues. Since tensions between two subunits of the organization and the need for clarification of responsibilities appeared to be the most pressing issues, a significant amount of time was spent on these matters. The first problem was addressed through a three-way intergroup exercise in which each of the major groups—the council, the tribal staff, and the Community Action Program staff—developed the following lists about the other two groups and shared them in a general session:

What we like about what the _____ group is doing.
What concerns us about the _____ group.
What we predict the _____ group will say about us.

During the sharing of the lists, discussion was limited to explanation and questions requesting clarification. This phase was followed by subgroup discussion and, finally, by total group discussion and action planning.

The problem of clarification of responsibilities was addressed by asking each participant to follow a suggested outline in writing his or her own job description, to make the descriptions visible on large newsprint, and to discuss the job descriptions with his or her particular work team, including the supervisor. Revised job descriptions were then posted in the general conference room for perusal and informal discussion during breaks in the sessions.

At the end of the workshop, the consultants, the council chairman, and the executive director agreed on the approximate date of two follow-up sessions at the tribal reservation and agreed to keep in touch by telephone.

ILLUSTRATION 5: A NEW PLANT MANAGER

Several years ago a new plant manager arrived at a continuous process facility (a plant where there is a continuous shaping of raw materials into finished products, like a steel-making plant or an oil refinery). He surveyed the scene and found the following characteristics: the plant had over two thousand employees; there were several layers of managers arranged in functional departments (production, maintenance, technical research, purchasing and stores, engineering, etc.); the plant performed fairly well in terms of productivity and profitability. The new manager's predecessor had been an energetic and autocratic man who had made all the operational and administrative decisions at the plant. The rest of the upper and middle management were called "super-intendents"—they superintended their bailiwicks, supplied information to the plant manager, and received orders from the manager about what should be done in their departments and divisions, as the plant was run on a day-to-day basis.

The new manager had a different managerial philosophy and a different leadership style: he believed in delegating as much responsibility to his subordinates as possible; he believed in allowing wide participation in the important decisions affecting the works and the work forces; he believed that better information and decisions would come from involved, committed "managers"; he wanted to develop subordinates so that they would move to higher positions of responsibility; and, as he told the managers at one of his first meetings with them, he wanted them to "share in the work and share in the fun." The new manager knew that he needed to build strong individual managers, an effective "management team," and that he needed to change the managerial culture and climate in the plant. He knew that this change in the way things were done would require new skills and a new management climate in the plant. And that would require training; the habits of ten years could not be changed just by his issuing an order. He called in several consultants, told them his desires, and solicited their aid.

As things evolved, there turned out to be six goals of the change project: (1) to increase the abilities and skills of the individual managers; (2) to build an effective top management team; (3) to build stronger division and department teams; (4) to improve the relations between work groups, such as between production and maintenance, and thus reduce the level of energy spent in competition; (5) to change the managerial culture from one in which one man made all the decisions to one in which all managers made or participated in decisions that affected them; and (6) to improve the long-range planning and decision-making abilities of managers at all levels. These change goals and the ideas of the new plant manager were public knowledge, just as was the information about the consultants and the OD program. Team-building meetings were held with the top management group and the new plant manager. Similar meetings were held with the division managers and their department manager subordinates. Meetings were held with the department managers and their supervisory subordinates. And finally, meetings were held with representatives from several "interface" groups—two or more interdependent groups with overlapping responsibilities or work flow duties. Also attending these meetings were the external consultants and several internal organization members who were being groomed as internal "change agents." The typical role of the consultants was to assist the groups to face up to, work through, and learn from their problems.

This OD program has been in operation for three years. During the first year the intervention strategy called mainly for family groups —intact working groups consisting of a superior and his key subordinates. These groups met to explore their culture and their methods of problem solving related to their assigned tasks within the organization. It was an important feature of the OD strategy that the first family group held involved the plant manager and his key subordinates, the plant division managers. Following this successful venture the division managers met with their subordinates in team-building sessions in an effort to improve division functioning. Significant issues surfaced during these meetings related to leadership styles, team processes and dynamics, and new ways of solving specific operational problems.

The second year's activities continued the team-building sessions and introduced a new dimension: interface meetings with groups that had problems working together. The fact that the groups had previously been successful in working on their own problems in family groups and analyzing their own dynamics seemed to facilitate the progress of the interface sessions. Greater understanding of the complexities of interdependence and the problems inherent in effective coordination of effort led to rapid and accurate diagnosis of the intergroup problems in most cases. Also during this year, OD task forces were formed to investigate various facets of effectively managing the plant. These task forces were typically temporary problem-solving teams with specific charges, but the charges had and continue to have far-reaching implications for the plant. For example, task forces have tackled industrial safety problems, labor and union relations issues, and external interface problems with the local community and region. An especially important task force outcome was the development of a new philosophy about career planning and also new career development planning and implementation procedures. These procedures provide better ways for utilizing and developing the manpower talent in the organization and also ensure the development of more managerial talent.

During the third year the top management team, including the plant manager, turned their attention to developing better long-range strategic planning models. They also instituted some management development programs for the purpose of upgrading the managerial skills of the middle-level supervisors. Some intergroup sessions continue to be utilized when conditions appear to warrant them. The family group sessions are primarily devoted to problem solving and long-range strategic planning.

CONCLUDING COMMENTS

These examples are not cited as perfect or ideal organizational interventions but only as fairly typical illustrations of what happens in organization development efforts. Although these programs vary in their comprehensiveness, all the illustrations have the following common features: (1) the "client" is a total system or major subunit of a total system; (2) the interventions are primarily directed toward problems and issues identified by the client group; (3) the interventions are directed toward problem solving and improved functioning for the client system; and (4) the interventions are based on behavioral science theory and technology.

In later chapters we will look more closely at many of the techniques, at the underlying theory and assumptions of OD, and at some of the pitfalls and challenges in attempting to improve organizations through behavioral science methods.

2

A Definition
of Organization Development

Although a literal interpretation of the words *organization development* could refer to a wide range of strategies for organization improvement, the phrase has come to take on some fairly specific meanings in the behavioral science literature and in practice. We say "fairly specific" because the boundaries are not entirely clear, perceptions of different authors and practitioners vary somewhat, and the field is evolving.

In the behavioral science, and perhaps ideal, sense of the term, *organization development is a long-range effort to improve an organization's problem-solving and renewal processes, particularly through a more effective and collaborative management of organization culture—with special emphasis on the culture of formal work teams—with the assistance of a change agent, or catalyst, and the use of the theory and technology of applied behavioral science, including action research.*

By *problem-solving processes* we mean the way an organization goes about diagnosing and making decisions about the opportunities and challenges of its environment. For example, does it see its environment, and thus its mission, in terms of ten years ago, or is it continuously redefining its purposes and its methods in terms of the present and the future? Does the organization solve problems in such a way that it taps the creativity and commitment of a select few, or does it tap deeply into the resources, vitality, and common purposes of all organizational members?

The notion of improving problem-solving processes is interrelated with the matter of improving organizational "renewal processes," which is perhaps a broader concept. Lippitt combines these ideas in his definition of *organization renewal* which he sees as

> the process of initiating, creating, and confronting needed changes so as to make it possible for organizations to become or remain viable, to

15

adapt to new conditions, to solve problems, to learn from experiences. . . .[1]

Argyris stresses organizational renewal and revitalizing in his description of organization development:

> At the heart of organizational development is the concern for the vitalizing, energizing, actualizing, activating, and renewing of organizations through technical and human resources.[2]

Similarly, Gardner, in writing about organizational *self-renewal,* refers to the avoidance of organizational decay and senility; the regaining of vitality, creativity, and innovation; the furtherance of flexibility and adaptability; the establishment of conditions that encourage individual motivation, development and fulfillment; and "the process of bringing results of change into line with purposes." [3] Thus, along with ideas about improved problem-solving and renewal processes are the important notions of purpose and direction—all of which are central to organization development activities.

By the term *culture* in our definition we mean prevailing patterns of activities, interactions, norms, sentiments (including feelings),[4] beliefs, attitudes, values, and products.[5] By including products we include technology in our definition, although changes in technology tend to be secondary in organization development efforts. However, technology—if one includes, procedures and methods along with equipment—is almost

---

[1] Gordon L. Lippitt, *Organization Renewal* (New York: Appleton-Century-Crofts, 1969), p. 1.

[2] Chris Argyris, *Management and Organizational Development: The Path from XA to YB* (New York: McGraw-Hill Book Company, 1971), p. ix.

[3] John W. Gardner, *Self-Renewal: The Individual and the Innovative Society* (New York: Harper & Row, Publishers, Harper Colophon Books, 1965), pp. 1–7.

[4] Whyte and Hamilton see sentiments as referring to "the mental and emotional reactions we have to people and physical objects" and as having three elements: "(1) An idea about something or somebody . . . , (2) emotional content or affect, (3) a tendency to recur upon presentation of the same symbols that have been associated with it in the past." William Foote Whyte and Edith Lentz Hamilton, *Action Research for Management* (Homewood, Ill.: Richard D. Irwin, Inc., 1965), p. 184.

[5] Kroeber and Kluckhohn cite 164 definitions of culture; our above definition is congruent with their synthesis: *"Culture consists of patterns, explicit and implicit, of and for behavior acquired and transmitted by symbols, constituting the distinctive achievement of human groups, including their embodiments in artifacts; the essential core of culture consists of traditional (i.e., historically derived and selected) ideas and especially their attached values; culture systems may, on the one hand, be considered as products of action, on the other as conditioning elements of further action."* See A. L. Kroeber and Clyde Kluckhohn, *Culture: A Critical Review of Concepts and Definitions* (New York: Vintage Books, 1952), pp. 291, 357.

always influenced, and is an influence, in organization development activities.

Our use of the term *culture* includes the˙ notion of the "informal system" which we will be describing in the next chapter as including feelings, informal actions and interactions, group norms, and values. In some ways the informal system is the hidden or suppressed domain of organizational life—the covert part of the "organizational iceberg," as shown in Figure 2-1.[6] Traditionally, this hidden domain either is not examined at all or is only partially examined. Organization development efforts focus on both the formal and the informal systems, but once the OD program is legitimated through the formal system, the initial intervention strategy is usually through the informal system in the sense that attitudes and feelings are usually the first data to be confronted.[7]

By *collaborative management* of the culture we mean a shared kind of management—not a hierarchically imposed kind. Who does what to whom is an important issue in organization development, and we want to stress that management of group culture must be "owned" as much by the subordinates as it is by the formal leader.

Our definition recognizes that the key unit in organization development activities is the ongoing work team, including both superior and subordinates. As we will elaborate upon in later chapters, this is different from more conventional ways of improving organizations. To give only one example, in most management development activities the focus is on the individual manager or supervisor—not on his work group. Traditionally he has participated in the learning experience in isolation from the dynamics of his work situation. Although we are emphasizing a focus on relatively permanent work groups to differentiate OD from traditional management development, in comprehensive OD programs extensive attention is also paid to temporary work teams, to overlapping team memberships, and to intergroup relations, as well as to total system implications. These matters will also be dealt with in subsequent chapters.

The notion of the use of a *change agent,* or *catalyst,* as one of the distinguishing characteristics of OD has a purpose in our definition. We

[6] This illustration is adapted from an address by Stanley N. Herman, TRW Systems Group, at an organization development conference sponsored jointly by the Industrial Relations Management Association of British Columbia and the NTL Institute for Applied Behavioral Science, Vancouver, B.C., Canada, 1970.

[7] Our use of the word *culture* includes Argyris's notion of the *living system:* "the way people actually behave, the way they actually think and feel, the way they actually deal with each other. It includes both the formal and informal activities." Chris Argyris, "Some Causes of Organizational Ineffectiveness within the Department of State," *Occasional Papers,* No. 2, Center for International Systems Research, U.S. Department of State, 1967, p. 2.

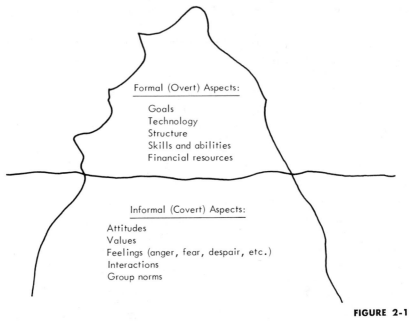

Formal (Overt) Aspects:

Goals
Technology
Structure
Skills and abilities
Financial resources

Informal (Covert) Aspects:

Attitudes
Values
Feelings (anger, fear, despair, etc.)
Interactions
Group norms

FIGURE 2-1

ORGANIZATIONAL ICEBERG

are somewhat pessimistic about the optimal effectiveness of OD efforts that are do-it-yourself programs. As will be discussed later, in the early phases, at least, the services of a third party who is not a part of the prevailing organization culture are essential. This does not mean that the third party cannot be a member of the organization but that he at least be external to the particular subsystem that is initiating an OD effort.

And finally, the basic intervention model which runs through most organization development efforts is *action research*. The action research model underlies all the illustrations of organization development described in the first chapter. Basically, the action research model consists of (1) a preliminary diagnosis, (2) data gathering from the client group, (3) data feedback to the client group, (4) data exploration by the client group, (5) action planning, and (6) action. This model will be discussed in detail in Chapter 8. Parenthetically, because of the extensive applicability of this model to organization development, another definition of *organization development* could be *organization improvement through action research*.

The above characteristics of organization development depart substantially from the features of traditional change programs, which Bennis categorizes as follows: " (1) exposition and propagation, (2) elite corps, (3) psychoanalytic insight, (4) staff, (5) scholarly consultations, and (6) circulation of ideas to the elite." [8] Bennis states that "exposition and propagation" are "possibly the most popular" and cites as illustrations the impact of the ideas of philosophers and scientists. The "elite corps" method is basically the infusion of scientists into key power and decision-making posts in organizations. "Psychoanalytic insight" as a change method is similar to the elite corps method but refers to effective change occurring through the medium of executives who have high self-insight and considerable "psychiatric wisdom" relative to subordinates. The "staff" strategy refers to the employment in organizations of social scientists who analyze situations and make policy recommendations. "Scholarly consultations" is a method of change involving "exploratory inquiry, scholarly understanding, scholarly confrontation, discovery of solutions, and, finally, scientific advice to the client." The sixth method described by Bennis is "circulation of ideas to the elite." One of the illustrations given is the Council of Correspondence, a chain letter which linked rebel leaders in the American Revolution.[9]

Organization development efforts depart substantially from these methods of organizational change. Of particular relevance are the two organizational consultation methods as categorized by Bennis, "staff" and "scholarly consultations." In both strategies an inside or an external expert studies a situation and makes recommendations; this is the traditional way of consulting. Organization development efforts are different. The OD consultant does *not* make recommendations in the traditional sense; he intervenes in the ongoing processes of the organization. For example, his end product is not a written report to top management, nor does he usually supply direct solutions to problems. He does, however, assist the client organization in the way it goes about solving problems. For example, he may be called upon to comment on the way a group is working together, or he may structure situations so as to highlight phenomena. As an illustration, if asked to assist in reducing conflict he may request two team members to role play each other and each other's point of view. But such interventions are in collaboration with the client group and are based on earned trust. Basically, he assists the client group in generating valid data and learning from them.

We see seven characteristics that we think differentiate organization development interventions from more traditional interventions:

1. An emphasis, although not exclusively so, on group and organizational processes in contrast to substantive content

---

[8] Warren G. Bennis, "A New Role for the Behavioral Sciences: Effecting Organizational Change," *Administrative Science Quarterly,* 8 (September 1963), 130.
[9] *Ibid.,* pp. 130–34.

2. An emphasis on the work team as the key unit for learning more effective modes of organizational behavior
3. An emphasis on the collaborative management of work team culture
4. An emphasis on the management of the culture of the total system and total system ramifications
5. The use of the *action research* model
6. The use of a behavioral scientist *change agent,* or catalyst
7. A view of the change effort as an ongoing process.

Another characteristic, number 8, a primary emphasis on human and social relationships, does not necessarily differentiate OD from other change efforts, but it is nevertheless an important feature.

These features will be elaborated upon in the chapters that follow. As we will see in the next chapter, these characteristics have identifiable origins in the very recent past and have emerged from the social sciences.

3

A History
of Organization Development

The history of organization development is rich with the contributions of behavioral scientists and practitioners, many of whom are well known, and the contributions of many people in client organizations. Even if we were aware of all the significant contributors, which we are not, we could not do justice to the richness of this history in a short chapter. Therefore, all we can do is to write about what we think are the central thrusts of that history and hope that the many people who are not mentioned will not be offended by our incompleteness.

We see systematic organization development activities as having a recent history, and to use an analogy with a tree, as having at least two important trunk stems. One stem consists of innovations in the application of laboratory-training insights to industrial organizations. A second major stem is survey research and feedback methodology. Both stems are intertwined with the history of action research, to which we will give some additional attention in Chapter 8.

THE LABORATORY-TRAINING STEM

One stem, laboratory training, essentially unstructured small-group situations in which participants learn from their own interactions and the evolving dynamics of the group, began to develop about 1946 from various experiments in the use of discussion groups to achieve changes in behavior in back-home situations. In particular, a workshop held at the State Teachers College in New Britain, Connecticut, in the summer of 1946 was important in the emergence of laboratory training. This workshop was sponsored by the Connecticut Interracial Commission and the Research Center for Group Dynamics, then at the Massachusetts Institute of

Technology. The leadership team for this action research consisted of Kurt Lewin, Kenneth Benne, Leland Bradford, and Ronald Lippitt. From this project emerged a three-week session during the summer of 1947 at Bethel, Maine, initially financed by the Office of Naval Research and sponsored by the National Education Association and the Research Center for Group Dynamics. The work of that summer was to evolve into the National Training Laboratories for Group Development and contemporary T-group training.[1]

Over the next decade, as trainers in the laboratory-training and group dynamics movement began to work with social systems of more permanency and complexity than T-groups, they began to experience considerable frustration in the transfer of laboratory behavioral skills and insights of individuals into the solution of problems in organizations. Personal skills learned in the "stranger" T-group setting were very difficult to transfer to complex organizations. However, the training of "teams" from the same organization had emerged early at Bethel and undoubtedly was a link to the total organizational focus of Douglas McGregor, Herbert Shepard, Robert Blake, and others.[2]

The late Douglas McGregor, working with Union Carbide beginning about 1957, was one of the first behavioral scientists to begin to solve the transfer problem and to talk systematically about and to help implement the application of laboratory-training skills to a complex organization.[3] In collaboration with McGregor, John Paul Jones, with the support of the Union Carbide's executive vice-president and director, Birny Mason, Jr. (later president of the corporation), established a small internal consulting group which in large part used behavioral science

---

[1] See Leland P. Bradford, Jack R. Gibb, and Kenneth D. Benne, *T-Group Theory and Laboratory Method* (New York: John Wiley & Sons, Inc., 1964), pp. 3, 81–83; and Alfred J. Marrow, *The Practical Theorist: The Life and Work of Kurt Lewin* (New York: Basic Books, 1969), pp. 210–14. For additional history see Leland P. Bradford, "Biography of an Institution," *Journal of Applied Behavioral Science,* 3 (April-May-June 1967), 127–43. For reference to the impact of John Dewey and others, see Bradford, Gibb, and Benne, *op. cit.,* especially p. 466. See also our chapter on "Action Research." We are indebted to Ronald Lippitt for his correspondence which helped clarify this and the following two paragraphs.

[2] Based on correspondence with Ronald Lippitt.

[3] Richard Beckhard, W. Warner Burke, and Fred I. Steele, "The Program for Specialists in Organization Training and Development," p. ii, mimeographed paper, NTL Institute for Applied Behavioral Science, December 1967; and John Paul Jones, "What's Wrong with Work?," in *What's Wrong with Work?* (New York: National Association of Manufacturers, 1967), p. 8. According to correspondence with Ronald Lippitt, as early as 1945, Leland Bradford and Ronald Lippitt were conducting "three-level training" at Freedman's Hospital in Washington, D.C., in an effort "to induce interdependent changes in all parts of the same system." Lippitt also reports that Leland Bradford very early was acting on a basic concept of "multiple entry," which is highly congruent with contemporary OD efforts.

knowledge in assisting line managers. Jones's organization was later called an "organization development group." [4]

During the same year, Herbert Shepard joined the Employee Relations Department of Esso Standard Oil as a research associate on organization. In 1958 and 1959 he launched three experiments in organization development at major Esso refineries: Bayonne, Baton Rouge, and Bayway. At Bayonne an interview survey and diagnosis were made and discussed with top management, followed by a series of three-day laboratories for all members of management. Paul Buchanan, who had been using a somewhat similar approach in Republic Aviation, collaborated with Shepard at Bayonne and subsequently joined the Esso staff. (Buchanan had previously been employed as a consulting psychologist by the Naval Ordnance Test Station at China Lake, California, where he had engaged the management in a number of activities, including "retreats" in which they worked on interpersonal relations.) [5]

At Baton Rouge, Robert Blake joined Shepard, and they initiated a series of two-week laboratories attended by all members of "middle" management. At first an effort was made to combine the case method with the laboratory method, but the designs soon became similar to NTL Institute's current Management Work Conferences which emphasize T-groups, organizational exercises, and lectures. One innovation in this training program was an emphasis on intergroup as well as interpersonal relations. Although working on interpersonal problems affecting work performance was clearly an organizational effort, between-group problem solving had even more organization development implications in that a broader and more complex segment of the organization was involved.

At Baton Rouge efforts to involve top management failed, and as a result follow-up resources for implementing organization development were not made available. By the time the Bayway program started two fundamental OD lessons had been learned: the requirement for active involvement in and leadership of the program by top management, and the need for on-the-job application.

At Bayway there were two significant innovations. First, Shepard, Blake, and Murray Horwitz utilized the instrumented laboratory, which Blake and Jane Mouton had been developing in social psychology classes at the University of Texas and which they later developed into the man-

---

[4] Gilbert Burck, "Union Carbide's Patient Schemers," *Fortune,* 72 (December 1965), 147–49. For McGregor's account, see "Team Building at Union Carbide," in Douglas McGregor, *The Professional Manager* (New York: McGraw-Hill Book Company, 1967), pp. 106–10.

[5] Much of the historical account in this paragraph and the following three paragraphs is based on correspondence with Herbert Shepard, with some information added from correspondence with Robert Blake.

agerial grid approach to organization development.[6] (An essential dimension of the instrumented lab is the use of feedback based on scales and measurements of group and individual behavior during sessions.) [7] Second, at Bayway more resources were devoted to team development, consultation, intergroup conflict resolution, and so forth, than were devoted to laboratory training of "cousins," that is, organization members from different departments.

As Robert Blake stated, "it was learning to *reject* T-group stranger-type labs that permitted OD to come into focus," and it was intergroup projects, in particular, that "triggered real OD." [8] As is evident from the Esso and the Union Carbide activities, Shepard, Blake, McGregor, and others were clearly trying to build on the insights and learnings of laboratory training toward more linkage with and impact on the problems and dynamics of ongoing organizations.

It is not entirely clear who coined the term *organization development,* but in all probability it was Robert Blake, Herbert Shepard, and Jane Mouton.[9] The phrase *development group* had earlier been used by Blake and Mouton in connection with human relations training at the University of Texas and appeared in their 1956 document "Training for Decision Making in Groups" which was distributed for use in connection with the Baton Rouge experiment.[10] (The same phrase appeared in a Mouton and Blake article first published in the journal *Group Psychotherapy* in 1957).[11] The Baton Rouge T-groups were called *development groups,*[12] and this terminology, coupled with the insights that were emerging, undoubtedly culminated in the concept of organization development.

It is of considerable significance that the emergence of organization

---

[6] Correspondence with Robert Blake and Herbert Shepard. For further reference to Murray Horwitz and Paul Buchanan, as well as comments about the innovative contributions of Michael Blansfield, see Herbert A. Shepard, "Explorations in Observant Participation," in Bradford, Gibb, and Benne, *T-Group Theory,* pp. 382–83.

[7] See Robert Blake and Jane Srygley Mouton, "The Instrumented Training Laboratory," in Irving R. Weschler and Edgar M. Schein, eds., *Selected Readings Series Five: Issues in Training* (Washington, D.C., National Training Laboratories, 1962), pp. 61–85. In this chapter, Blake and Mouton credit Muzafer and Carolyn Sherif with important contributions to early intergroup experiments. Reference is also made to the contributions of Frank Cassens of Humble Oil and Refinery in the early phases of the Esso program.

[8] Based on correspondence with Robert Blake.

[9] Blake correspondence.

[10] Blake correspondence.

[11] Jane Srygley Mouton and Robert R. Blake, "University Training in Human Relations Skills," *Selected Readings Series Three: Forces in Learning* (Washington, D.C.: National Training Laboratories, 1961), pp. 88–96, reprinted from *Group Psychotherapy,* 10 (1957), 342–45.

[12] Shepard and Blake correspondence.

development efforts in the first two corporations to be involved, Union Carbide and Esso, included employee relations–industrial relations people seeing themselves in new roles. At Union Carbide, John Paul Jones, who had come up through industrial relations, now saw himself in the role of behavioral science consultant to other managers.[13] At Esso, the headquarters human relations research division began to view itself as an internal consulting group offering services to field managers rather than as a research group developing reports for top management.[14] Thus, in the history of OD we see both external consultants and internal staff departments departing from traditional roles and collaborating in quite a new approach to organization improvement.

THE SURVEY RESEARCH FEEDBACK STEM

Of particular importance to the history of organization development is a specialized form of action research which we will call *survey research and feedback*, which refers to the use of attitude surveys and data feedback in workshop sessions. Survey research and feedback constitutes the second major stem in the history of organization development.

The history of this stem, in particular, revolves around the experience staff members at the Research Center for Group Dynamics, founded in 1945 by Kurt Lewin, were gaining over a period of years in *action research* (see Chapter 8). The Center was first established at the Massachusetts Institute of Technology; after Lewin's death in 1947, the senior staff moved to the University of Michigan to join with Michigan's Survey Research Center to form the Institute for Social Research. A few of the key figures involved at M.I.T. in addition to Lewin were Marian Radke, Leon Festinger, Ronald Lippitt, Douglas McGregor, John R. P. French, Jr., Dorwin Cartwright, and Morton Deutsch.[15] Names conspicuous in the work at Michigan in recent years include Floyd Mann and Rensis Likert.

As one example in 1948 at the Detroit Edison Company, researchers began systematic feedback of data from a company-wide employee and

[13] Burck, "Union Carbide's Patient Schemers," p. 149.
[14] Harry D. Kolb, "Introduction" to *An Action Research Program for Organization Improvement* (Ann Arbor: Foundation for Research on Human Behavior, 1960), p. i. The phrase *organization development* is used several times in this monograph based on a 1959 meeting about the Esso programs and written by Kolb, Shepard, Blake, and others.
[15] For part of this history, see Marrow, *The Practical Theorist*, Chap. 19, and *A Quarter Century of Social Research*, Institute for Social Research, 1971.

management attitude survey.[16] In this project, data from an attitude survey were fed back in participating accounting departments in what Mann calls an "interlocking chain of conferences."[17] (This project will be discussed in more detail in Chapter 12.) Some of the insights that emerged from this process have a very contemporary OD ring. To illustrate, in drawing conclusions from the Detroit Edison study, Baumgartel stated:

> The results of this experimental study lend support to the idea that an intensive, group discussion procedure for utilizing the results of an employee questionnaire survey can be an effective tool for introducing positive change in a business organization. It may be that the effectiveness of this method, in comparison to traditional training courses, is that it deals with the system of human relationships as a whole (superior and subordinate can change together) and it deals with each manager, supervisor, and employee in the context of his own job, his own problems, and his own work relationships.[18]

KURT LEWIN

If laboratory training and survey research constitute the two main stems in the organization development tree, then certainly Kurt Lewin's work in developing a field theory of social psychology was the taproot. His passionate interest in applied behavioral science was the main thrust to both laboratory training and survey research. Lewin was a central figure in the origin of both the National Training Laboratories (now NTL–Institute for Applied Behavioral Science) and the Research Center for Group Dynamics. Although Lewin died only two years after the founding of the Research Center and just before the first formal session of NTL, he had a profound influence on both organizations and the people associated with them, and his influence continues today.[19]

---

[16] Floyd C. Mann, "Studying and Creating Change," in Warren Bennis, Kenneth Benne, and Robert Chin, *The Planning of Change* (New York: Holt, Rinehart & Winston, Inc., 1961), pp. 605–13. Another early project which had some overtones of organization development but was not published for many years was the "Tremont Hotel Project." See William Foote Whyte and Edith Lentz Hamilton, *Action Research for Management* (Homewood, Ill.: Richard D. Irwin, Inc., 1965), pp. 1–282.

[17] Mann, "Studying and Creating Change," p. 609.

[18] Howard Baumgartel, "Using Employee Questionnaire Results for Improving Organizations: The Survey 'Feedback' Experiment," *Kansas Business Review*, 12 (December 1959), 2–6.

[19] For an excellent and detailed account of Lewin's life and influence, see Marrow, *The Practical Theorist*, Parts I–III. This book is rich with events that are important in the history of OD. For example, Marrow mentions a 1944 dinner that Rensis Likert arranged so that Douglas McGregor and Kurt Lewin could explore the feasibility of a group dynamics center at M.I.T. (p. 164).

EXTENT OF APPLICATION

Applications emerging from one or both of the two stems above are evident in the organization development efforts that are becoming visible in many countries, including England, Japan, Norway, Canada, Sweden, Australia, and Holland, as well as in the United States. Just a few of the growing number of organizations in America that have embarked on organization development efforts are Union Carbide and Esso (the first two companies), I.B.M., Hotel Corporation of America, National Aeronautics and Space Administration (NASA), Boise Cascade, Polaroid, Armour and Company, Texas Instruments, American Airlines, and TRW Systems Group. Applications at TRW, a large research and development organization in the aerospace field, commenced in 1961 and may be as extensive and innovative as those found anywhere in the world.[20] Efforts there have included laboratory training, team building, interface laboratories between departments and between company and customers, and career planning. In England and Europe, illustrative of growing interest in organization development is the involvement of such companies as Imperial Chemical Industries, J. Lyons & Company, and the Shell Oil Company. Projects at Imperial Chemical Industries, a large company headquartered in London, have included job enrichment, survey research, and team-building approaches.

Industrial organizations, however, are by no means the only kinds of institutions involved, as we indicated by the illustrations in Chapter 1. We know of applications, for example, in public school systems, colleges, social welfare agencies, police departments, governmental departments, and churches and in certain American Indian tribes.

Some "community development" strategies have a number of elements in common with organization development, for example, the use of action research, the use of a change agent, and an emphasis on facilitating decision-making and problem-solving processes.[21] Undoubtedly, some of the commonality stems from OD practitioners working in the community development field. For example, in 1961 Herbert Shepard conducted community development laboratories at China Lake, California, sponsored by

[20] See Sheldon A. Davis, "An Organic Problem-Solving Method of Organizational Change," *Journal of Applied Behavioral Science*, 3 (November 1, 1967), 3–21. See also the case study of TRW Systems Group in Gene Dalton, Paul Lawrence, and Larry Greiner, *Organizational Change and Development* (Homewood, Ill.: Irwin-Dorsey Press, 1970), pp. 104–53.

[21] See the discussion of *locality development* by Jack Ruthman, "Three Models of Community Organization Practice," in Fred M. Cox, ed., *Strategies of Community Organization: A Book of Readings* (Itasca, Ill.: F. E. Peacock, 1970), pp. 20–36.

the Naval Ordnance Test Station. These labs were week long and involved military persons and civilians and people of all ages and socioeconomic levels. Outcomes included the resolution of some community and intercommunity issues.[22] Similarly, some OD-type change efforts have focused on what are clearly interorganization systems. For example, we know of one change effort involving police, prosecutors, judges, institutional personnel, and parole officers as a *system*.

In addition to emphasizing the diversity of types of systems with which OD consultants have worked, we want to emphasize that intra-organization development efforts have not focused on just top management teams, although the importance of top management involvement will be discussed in later chapters. A wide range of occupational roles has been involved, including work groups of scientists and engineers; production workers; [23] other professionals such as lawyers, accountants, and computer specialists; and technicians, secretaries, and clerical employees.

Symptomatic of the widespread application of organization development concepts is the emergence and growth of the OD Network of NTL–Institute for Applied Behavioral Science which began in 1964 and now has a membership of over two hundred. Most members either have major roles in the OD efforts of organizations or are scholars in the OD field. An OD Division of the American Society of Training and Development started in 1968 and had close to eight hundred members toward the end of 1970.[24]

It is also significant that in 1971 the Academy of Management, whose members are mostly professors in management and related areas, began a Division of Organization Development within its structure. An organizing meeting was held in Atlanta, Georgia, in connection with the academy's annual meeting. That same year the Division of Industrial and Organizational Psychology of the American Psychological Association included a workshop on organization development in the annual APA convention; several annual conventions going back to at least 1965 had included papers or symposia on organization development or related topics.[25]

The first doctoral program devoted to training OD specialists was

---

[22] Shepard correspondence. Starting with 1967, Herbert Shepard was involved in the applications of OD to community problems in Middletown, Connecticut.

[23] See Scott Myers, "Overcoming Union Opposition to Job Enrichment," *Harvard Business Review,* 49 (May–June 1971), 37–49; and Robert Blake, Herbert Shepard, and Jane Mouton, *Managing Intergroup Conflict in Industry* (Houston: Gulf Publishing Company, 1964,) pp. 122–38.

[24] Forrest R. Belcher, "A Report on ASTD's 1970 Accomplishments," *Training and Development Journal,* 25 (March 1971), 9.

[25] For example, the following topics were included in the program of the 1965 convention: "Strategies for Organization Improvement: Research and Consultation," "Managerial Grid Organization Development," and "The Impact of Laboratory Training in a Research and Development Environment," *American Psychologist,* 20 (July 1965), 549, 562, 565.

founded by Herbert Shepard in 1960 at the Case Institute of Technology. First called "The Organizational Behavior Group," this program is now part of the Department of Organization and Administration of Case-Western Reserve. In addition, we know of at least the following additional universities having graduate courses directly bearing on organization development: Harvard, M.I.T., UCLA, and Yale. A number of universities, such as the University of Washington, are just beginning to add courses in organization development to their graduate curricula.

Giving major impetus to this rapid growth in interest and attention has been NTL's Program for Specialists in Organization Training and Development, which is an intensive, month-long session held in the summer. A major part of this program is devoted to consultation skills. The first such program was held in 1967 in Bethel, Maine, as an outgrowth of an Organization Intern Program which had included some OD training. In subsequent years, programs have been offered in two locations. Other shorter programs are beginning to appear under the sponsorship of NTL Institute, universities and foundations, and other institutions.

CONCLUDING COMMENTS

Organization development has emerged from applied behavioral science and social psychology and from subsequent efforts to apply laboratory training and survey feedback insights into total systems. Its history is emergent in that a rapidly increasing number of behavioral scientists and practitioners in organizations are building on the research and insights of the past as well as discovering the utility of some of the earlier insights. These efforts are beginning to be widespread and include a wide range of organizations, types of institutions, levels of employees, and geographical locations. In the chapters that follow, its assumptions and techniques will be examined in substantial depth along with some speculations as to its future viability.

The Theory and Practice of Organization Development

operational components

characteristics and foundations

assumptions and values

relevant systems concepts

action research

OD interventions:
an overview

OD interventions:
a descriptive inventory

conditions for success

4

the nature of organization development
Operational Components

Organization development, defined in Chapter 2 and differentiated from other organizational and educational interventions, is a unique process for improving organizational functioning. In this chapter and the next we continue and extend that earlier discussion in order to provide a more thorough understanding of the nature of OD. The efficacy of organizational development is due partly to the nature of the OD process itself, and that is what we explore in chapters 4 and 5. The nature of OD—what it is, what it tries to accomplish, what it is in concrete applications and abstract formulations, what characteristics and components it has, and what its theoretical underpinnings are—that is the scope of this discussion.

The nature of OD could be presented in several ways. As shown in Figure 4-1, we have chosen to characterize it in terms of the *foundations* of the OD process and the *components of the OD process in operation*. The outer ellipse describes the foundation characteristics we consider important; the inner ellipse describes the basic components (or operations) found in any OD program.

First, three basic components of the OD process in operation are examined. Any OD program will contain these elements of diagnosis, action, and process-maintenance. Second, the major characteristics and the theoretical underpinnings of organization development are explored; these might be considered the foundation upon which the process is built. The characteristics we want particularly to emphasize are that organization development is an ongoing interactive process, is data based (built on an action research model), is experience based, is goal oriented, constitutes a normative–re-educative strategy of changing, is both a form of and a result of applied behavioral science, uses a systems approach, and has a work team emphasis. Some facets of the characteristics are treated more ex-

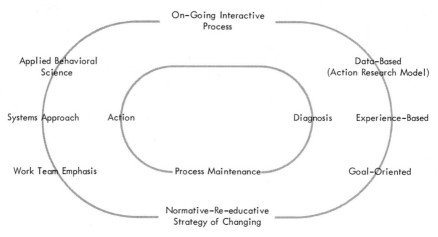

(Outer Ellipse shows the Foundations of the OD Process; Inner Ellipse shows
the Components of the OD Process in Operation)

FIGURE 4-1

THE NATURE OF ORGANIZATION DEVELOPMENT

tensively in other sections of the book, but we deal with them all here to
show the broad base of organization development as a process of planned
change.

BASIC COMPONENTS OF AN OD PROGRAM

Implementation of an OD program requires attention to three operations that we call the basic components or elements of an OD program in
operation: the diagnostic component, representing a continuous collection
of system data, focuses on the total system, its subsystems, and system
processes; the action (or intervention) component consists of all the
activities of consultants and system members designed to improve the
organization's functioning; [1] and the process-maintenance component en-
compasses the activities oriented toward the maintenance and management
of the OD process itself. The first two elements relate to the OD process
vis-à-vis the organization; the third element relates to the OD process
vis-à-vis itself.

[1] In fact, all three components represent actions or interventions in the system
and thus fall into an action category. Diagnostic activities, for example, have a
powerful "action impact" on an organization. We have artificially separated the
three components here for analytical purposes only.

THE DIAGNOSTIC COMPONENT: DIAGNOSING THE SYSTEM AND ITS
PROCESSES

OD is at heart an action program based on valid information about
the *status quo,* current problems and opportunities, and effects of actions
as they relate to goal achievement. An OD program thus starts with diagnosis and continuously employs data collecting and data analyzing throughout. The requirement for diagnostic activities—activities designed to
provide an accurate account of things as they really are—stems from two
needs: the first need is to know the state of things, or "what is"; the
second need is to know the effects or consequences of actions.

The importance of diagnostic activities is emphasized by Beckhard
as follows:

> The development of a strategy for systematic improvement of an organi-
> zation demands an examination of the present state of things. Such an
> analysis usually looks at two broad areas. One is a diagnosis of the
> various subsystems that make up the total organization. These subsys-
> tems may be natural "teams" such as top management, the production
> department, or a research group; or they may be levels such as top
> management, middle management, or the work force.
> The second area of diagnosis is the organization processes that are
> occurring. These include decision-making processes, communications pat-
> terns and styles, relationships between interfacing groups, the manage-
> ment of conflict, the setting of goals, and planning methods.[2]

Table 4-1 shows how one would proceed to diagnose a system and its
subsystems (the whole and its subunits). For each of the major targets or
subsystems in an organization, the typical information desired and common
methods of obtaining the information are given. The OD practitioner may
be interested in all these target groups or only in one or two of them; he
may work with one subsystem during one phase of the program and other
subsystems during subsequent phases. Frequently the improvement strategy
(the overall OD intervention strategy) calls for concentrating on different
organizational targets in a planned sequence. For example, the program
may start at an important subsystem, move to another subsystem, and then
extend to the total organization; or the initial focus could be on the total
organization and then move to selected subsystems. Some of the critical

---

[2] Richard Beckhard, *Organization Development: Strategies and Models* (Reading, Mass.: Addison-Wesley Publishing Company, 1969), p. 26. Beckhard's use of
subsystem synonymously with *subunit* is congruent with our usage in Chapter 7.
However, we develop a supplemental conceptual scheme in that chapter that also
permits viewing the organization in terms of subsystems that are common to all
subunits: goal, technological, task, structural, human-social, and external interface.

TABLE 4-1

DIAGNOSING ORGANIZATIONAL SUBSYSTEMS

Diagnostic Focus or Target	Explanation and Identifying Examples	Typical Information Sought	Common Methods of Diagnosis
The total organization (having a common "charter" or mission and a common power structure)	The total system is the entity assessed and analyzed. The diagnosis might also include, if relevant, extrasystem (environmental) organizations, groups, or forces, such as customers, suppliers, and governmental regulations. Examples are a manufacturing firm, a hospital, a school system, a department store chain, or a church denomination.	What are the norms ("cultural oughts") of the organization? What is the organization's culture? What are the attitudes, opinions, and feelings of system members toward various "cognitive objects" such as compensation, organization goals, supervision, and top management? What is the organization climate—open vs. closed, authoritarian vs. democratic, repressive vs. developmental, trusting vs. suspicious, cooperative vs. competitive? How well do key organizational processes, such as decision making and, goal setting, function? What kind and how effective are the organization's "sensing mechanisms" to monitor internal and external demands? Are organization goals understood and accepted?	Questionnaire surveys are most popular with a large organization. Interviews, both group and individual, are useful for getting detailed information, especially if based on effective sampling techniques. A panel of representative members who are surveyed or interviewed periodically is useful to chart changes over time. Examination of organizational "potsherds"—rules, regulations, policies, symbols of office and/or status, etc., yields insight into the organization's culture. Diagnostic meetings held at various levels within the organization yield a great amount of information in a short time period.
Large subsystems that are by nature complex and heterogeneous	This target group stems from making different "slices" of the organization, such as by hierarchical level, junction, and geographical location. Two criteria help to identify this set of subsystems: first they are viewed as a subsystem by themselves or others; and second, they are heterogeneous in makeup, that is, the members have some things in common, but many differences from each other, too. Examples would be the middle management group, consisting of managers from diverse functional groups; the personnel department members of an organization that has widely dispersed operations with a personnel group at each location; everyone in one plant in a company that has ten plants; a division made up of several functional groups.	All of the above, plus: how does this subsystem view the whole and vice versa? How do the members of this subsystem get along together? What are the unique demands on this subsystem? Are organization structures and processes related to the unique demands? Are there "high" and "low" subunits within the subsystem in terms of performance? Why? What are the major problems confronting this subsystem and its subunits? Are the subsystem's goals compatible with organization goals? Does the heterogeneity of role demands and functional identity get in the way of effective subsystem performance?	If the subsystems are large or widely dispersed, questionnaire and survey techniques are recommended. Interviews and observations may be used to provide additional supporting or hypothesis-testing information.

Target subsystem	Description	Diagnostic questions	Methods
Small subsystems that are simple and relatively homogeneous	These are typically formal work groups or teams that have frequent face-to-face interaction. They may be permanent groups, temporary task forces, or newly constituted groups (e.g., the group charged with the "start-up" of a new operation, or the group formed by an acquisition or merger). Examples are the top management team, any manager and his key subordinates, committees of a permanent or temporary nature, task force teams, the work force in an office, the teachers in a single school, etc.	The questions on culture, climate, attitudes, and feelings are relevant here, plus: What are the major problems of the team? How can team effectiveness be improved? What do people do that gets in the way of others? Are member/leader relations those that are desired? Do individuals know how their jobs relate to group and organizational goals? Are the group's working processes, i.e., the way they get things done as a group, effective? Is good use made of group and individual resources?	Typical methods include the following: individual interviews followed by a group meeting to review the interview data; short questionnaires; observation of staff meetings and other day-to-day operations; and a family group meeting for self-diagnosis.
Small, total organizations that are relatively simple and homogeneous	An example would be a local professional organization. Typical problems might be declining membership, low attendance, or difficulty in manning special task forces.	How do the officers and the members see the organization and its goals? What do they like and dislike about it? What do they want it to be like? What is the competition like? What significant external forces are impacting on the organization?	Questionnaires or interviews are frequently used. Descriptive adjective questionnaires can be used to obtain a quick reading on the culture, "tone," and health of the organization.
Interface or inter-group subsystems	These consist of subsets of the total system that contain members of two subsystems, such as a matrix organizational structure requiring an individual or a group to have two reporting lines. But more often this target consists of members of one subsystem having common problems and responsibilities with members of another subsystem. We mean to include subsystems with common problems and responsibilities such as production and maintenance overlaps, marketing and sales overlaps.	How does each subsystem see the other? What problems do the two groups have in working together? In what ways do the subsystems get in each other's way? How can they collaborate to improve the performance of both groups? Are goals, subgoals, areas of authority and responsibility clear? What is the nature of the climate between the groups? What do the members want it to be?	Confrontation meetings between both groups are often the method for data gathering and planning corrective actions. Organization mirroring meeting is used when three or more groups are involved. Interviews of each subsystem followed by a "sharing the data" meeting or observation of interactions can be used.
Dyads and/or Triads	Superior/subordinate pairs, interdependent peers, linking pins—i.e., persons who have multiple group memberships—all these are subsystems worthy of analysis.	What is the quality of the relationship? Do the parties have the necessary skills for task accomplishment? Are they collaborative or competitive? Are they effective as a subsystem? Does the addition of a third party facilitate or inhibit their progress? Are they supportive of each other?	Separate interviews followed by a meeting of the parties to view any discrepancies in the interview data are often used. Checking their perceptions of each other through confrontation situations may be useful. Observation is an important way to assess the dynamic quality of the interaction.

TABLE 4-1 (Continued)

Diagnostic Focus or Target	Explanation and Identifying Examples	Typical Information Sought	Common Methods of Diagnosis
Individuals	Any individual within the organization, such as president, division heads, key occupants of positions in a work flow process, e.g., quality control, R & D. In school systems, this would be (a) students, (b) teachers, or (c) administrators.	Does he perform according to the organization's expectations? How does he view his place and performance? Do certain kinds of problems typically arise? Does he meet standards and norms of the organization? Does he need particular knowledge, skills, or ability? What career development opportunities does he have/want/need? What pain is he experiencing?	Interviews, information derived from diagnostic work team meetings, or problems identified by personnel department are sources of information. Self-assessment growing out of team or subsystem interventions is another source.
Roles	A role is a set of behaviors enacted by a person as a result of his occupying a certain position within the organization. All persons in the organization have roles requiring certain behaviors, such as the secretaries, production foremen, accountants.	Should the role behaviors be added to, subtracted from, or changed? Is the role defined adequately? What is the "fit" between the person and his role? Should the role performer be given special skills and knowledge? Is this the right person for this role?	Usually information comes from observations, interviews, role analysis technique, a team approach to "management by objectives." Career planning activities yield this information as an output.
Between organization systems constituting a supra system	An example might be the system of law and order in a region, including local, county, state, federal police or investigative and enforcement agencies, courts, prisons, parole agencies, prosecuting officers and grand juries. Most such supra systems are so complex that change efforts tend to focus on a pair or a trio of subparts.	How do the key people in one segment of the supra system view the whole and the subparts? Are there frictions or incongruities between subparts? Are there high-performing and low-performing subunits? Why?	Organizational mirroring, or developing lists of how each group sees each other, is a common method of joint diagnosis. Questionnaires and interviews are useful in extensive, long-range interventions.

issues and dimensions concerning how, when, and where to begin the OD program will be covered in later chapters.

An alternative way to conceptualize the diagnostic component emphasizes the organization's principal processes rather than its primary target groups. Such a scheme is presented in Table 4-2 showing the principal organization processes, the typical desired information concerning the processes, and the common methods of obtaining the information.

In practice the OD consultant works from both tables simultaneously. Although he is interested in some specific target group from Table 4-1 and the information about that group, he is also interested in the processes found in that group and would rely on Table 4-2. Organizational processes are the *what* and the *how* of the organization, that is, What is going on? and How is it being accomplished? To know about the organization's processes is to know about the organization in its dynamic and complex reality. OD practitioners typically pay special attention to the processes listed in Table 4-2 because of their centrality for effective organization functioning, because of their ubiquitous nature in organizations, and because significant organizational problems often stem from them. Careful examination of the two tables will give a good sense of the inner workings of an OD program and its thrusts, emphases, and mechanics.

These tables are intended as heuristic tools for operational diagnosis. As an illustration, say the personnel director in conjunction with a manager of a large, complex, heterogeneous subsystem is interested in OD efforts primarily directed to improving the functioning of significant pairs and individuals within the subsystem. It is helpful to know what information is typically needed and what methods are available for getting an accurate picture of the *status quo* of the large complex unit. And it is helpful to know what different kinds of information and data-gathering techniques are indicated when attention is focused on the pairs and individuals. This knowledge facilitates designing the diagnostic phase of the organization development program.

Finally, in an OD program, not only are the *results* of diagnostic activities important, but *how the information is collected* and *what is done with the information* are also significant aspects of the process. There is active collaboration between the OD practitioner and the organization members about such issues as what target groups are to be diagnosed, how the diagnosis is best accomplished, what processes and dynamics should be analyzed, what is to be done with the information, how the data will be worked with, and how the information will be used to aid action planning. We believe these features of the OD process are directly and causally related to the efficacy of organization development as a change technique.

TABLE 4-2

DIAGNOSING ORGANIZATIONAL PROCESSES

Organizational Process	Identifying Remarks and Explanation	Typical Information Sought	Common Methods of Diagnosis
Communications patterns, styles and flows.	Who talks to whom, for how long, about what? Who initiates the interaction? Is it two-way or one-way? Is it top-down; down-up; lateral?	Is communication directed upward, downward, or both? Are communications filtered? Why? In what way? Do communications patterns "fit" the nature of the jobs to be accomplished? What is the "climate" of communications? What is the place of written communications vs. verbal?	Observations, especially in meetings; questionnaires for large-size samples; interviews and discussions with group members—all these methods may be used to collect the desired information.
Goal setting	Setting task objectives and determining criteria to measure accomplishment of the objectives takes place at all organizational levels.	Do they set goals? How is this done? Who participates in goal setting? Do they possess the necessary skills for effective goal setting? Are they able to set long-range and short-range objectives?	Questionnaires, interviews, and observation all afford ways of assessing goal-setting ability of individuals and groups within the organization.
Decision making, problem solving, and action planning	Evaluating alternatives and choosing a plan of action are an integral and central function for most organization members. This includes getting the necessary information, establishing priorities, evaluating alternatives, and choosing one alternative over all others.	Who makes decisions? Are they effective? Are all available resources utilized? Are additional decision-making skills needed? Are additional problem-solving skills needed? Are organization members satisfied with the problem-solving and decision-making processes?	Observation of problem-solving meetings at various organizational levels is particularly valuable in diagnosing this process.
Conflict resolution and management	Conflict—interpersonal, intrapersonal, and intergroup—frequently exists in organizations. Does the organization have effective ways of dealing with conflict?	Where does conflict exist? Who are the involved parties? How is it being managed? What are the system norms for dealing with conflict? Does the reward system promote conflict?	Interviews, third-party observations, and observation of group meetings are common methods for diagnosing these processes.
Managing interface relations	Interfaces represent these situations wherein two or more groups (subsystems) face common problems or overlapping responsibility. This is most often seen when members of two separate groups are interdependently related in achieving an objective but have separate accountability.	What is the nature of the relations between the two groups? Are goals clear? Is responsibility clear? What major problems do the two groups face?	Interviews, third-party observations, and observation of group meetings are common methods for diagnosing these processes.
Superior-subordinate relations	Formal hierarchical relations in organizations dictate that some people lead and others follow; these situations are often a source of many organizational problems.	What are the extant leadership styles? What problems arise between superiors and subordinates?	Questionnaires can show overall leadership climate and norms. Interviews and questionnaires reveal the desired leadership behaviors.

THE ACTION COMPONENT: INTERVENING IN THE CLIENT SYSTEM

As we have seen, organization development may be viewed as a process designed to improve an organization's adapting, coping, problem-solving, and goal-setting processes. This is accomplished by activities in the client system called *interventions* which we define in Chapter 9 as *"sets of structured activities* in which selected organizational units (target groups or individuals) engage with a task or sequence of tasks where the task goals are *related directly or indirectly to organizational improvement."* Planning actions, executing actions, and evaluating the consequences of actions are an integral and essential part of most OD interventions.

This emphasis on action planning and action taking is a powerful feature of OD and, in some respects, is a distinguishing one. In many traditional educational and training activities, learning and action taking are separated in that the knowledge and skills are "learned" in one setting, say, in a classroom, and are then taken back to the organization with the learner being admonished to practice what he has learned, that is, to take actions. This artificial separation is minimized in most OD interventions in several ways. First, in many intervention activities there are two goals: a learning or educational goal and an accomplishing-a-task goal. Second, OD problem-solving interventions tend to focus on real organizational problems that are central to the needs of the organization rather than on hypothetical, abstract problems that may or may not fit the members' needs. Third, OD interventions utilize several learning models, not just one. Let us examine these three points in more detail.

The dual aspect of OD interventions can be clarified with an illustration. Let us say that the top executives of an organization spend three days together in a workshop in which they do the following things: (1) explore the need for and desirability of a long-range strategy plan for the organization; (2) learn how to formulate such a strategy by analyzing other strategies, determining what the strategic variables are, being shown a sequence of steps for preparing a comprehensive plan, and so forth; and (3) actually make a three-year strategy plan for the organization.[3] This intervention combines the dual features of learning and action: the executives engaged in activities in which they learned about strategy planning, and they then generated a strategy. In some OD interventions, the "learning aspect" predominates, and in others, the "action aspect" predominates; but both aspects are present in most interventions.

[3] Actually, in a real strategy-planning session steps 1 and 2 might take place during the first session, with that session concluding with some "homework" assignments to the members in order that the necessary information for the strategy plan could be available. Then, in a second session, step 3 would be finalized. This kind of separation in time is not the artificial one described above, but a separation in time designed to facilitate step 3.

OD interventions tend to focus on real problems rather than on abstract problems. The problems facing organization members are real, not hypothetical; the problems members get rewarded for solving are real, not hypothetical; and the problems central to the needs of organization members are real, not hypothetical. Developing the skills and knowledge to solve real problems as they arise in their "natural state" means that the educational problem of "transfer of learning" from one situation to another is minimized (although the problem of generalization, that is, knowing the appropriate times and places to apply this particular set of skills and knowledge, is still present).

An additional feature of working on real problems, as found in some OD interventions, is that the real set of individuals involved in the problem is the group that the problem solvers work with. For example, in a human relations class, if a manager was having trouble understanding and working with disadvantaged subordinates, he would perhaps "role play" the situation with his instructor or fellow students. In OD he would probably interact with the disadvantaged employees he was having difficulties with —but he would do so in carefully structured activities that have a high probability of resulting in learning for both parties and a high probability of being a "success experience" for both parties.

Organization development programs rely on several learning models. For example, if "learning how to" do something precedes "doing" it, then we have a somewhat traditional approach to learning that most people are familiar with. If the "doing" precedes the "learning how to," then we have a "deficiency" model of learning in which the learning comes primarily from critiquing the actions after the fact to see how they could have been done differently and, presumably, better. Both models are viable learning modes, and both are used extensively in organization development. Even the traditional model of "learning how to" and "doing" becomes nontraditional as performed in OD, however, since the OD approach would be for a formal work team to be learning and doing *together* with the help of a change agent.

Action programs in OD are closely linked with explicit goals and objectives. Careful attention is given to the problem of translating goals into observable, explicit, and measurable actions or behaviors, and equal care is given to the related problem of ensuring that actions are relevant to and instrumental for goal attainment. Such questions as the following thus become an integral part of organizational life: How does this action relate to the goal we have established? What are the action implications of that goal for me, my subordinates, my group? When we say we want to achieve a certain goal, what do we really mean by that, in measurable terms? Given several alternative forms of action, which one seems most appropriate to achieve the goal we have set?

Diagnosis, action taking, and goal setting are inextricably related in an OD program. Diagnostic activities are precursors to action programs, that is, fact-finding is done to provide a foundation for action. Actions are continuously evaluated for their contribution to goal accomplishment. Goals are continuously evaluated in terms of their appropriateness— whether or not they are attainable and whether or not they can be translated into action programs. These three components of OD are also the basic components of the action research model, and it is for this reason that we view OD as "organization improvement through action research." Organization development is a continuous process of the cycling of setting goals and objectives, collecting data about the *status quo,* planning and taking actions based on hypotheses and on the data, and evaluating the effects of action through additional data collection.

Chapters 9 through 13 describe the range, scope, and details of the majority of OD interventions, and for that reason we defer additional elaboration of the action component of OD until then.

THE PROCESS-MAINTENANCE COMPONENT:
MAINTAINING AND MANAGING THE OD PROCESS ITSELF

Just as OD practitioners apply behavioral science principles and practices to ongoing complex systems in order to improve the system's functioning, ideally they apply these same principles and practices to their own work. The OD process and the practitioner group typically model the techniques being proposed for the organization; both the program and the practitioners practice what they preach. Diagnosing and evaluating are an integral part of managing the OD process, similarly so is treating the organization from a systems viewpoint with the OD program being a component force within a wider field of system forces. Practitioners would find the client system probably resisting their teaching and preachings about the desirability and feasibility of managing interpersonal conflict if it were known that conflict was not being managed within the OD group; teaching others to manage against measurable objectives would appear hollow if the OD group did not know where it was going and how; reverberations will occur throughout the total organization as a result of an OD program in one subsystem and this fact must be taken into account.

Among other things, managing the OD process means actively seeking answers to the following questions:

Are we being timely and relevant in our interventions?
Are our activities producing the effects we intended and wanted? If not, why not; if so, why?

Is there continued "ownership," that is, involvement, commitment, and investment, in the program by the clients?

What are the total system ramifications of our efforts? Did we anticipate these? Are any of the ramifications undesirable? If yes, what do we do about them?

What about the culture of our own OD group? Must it be changed in any ways? Are we solving problems effectively, managing against clearly understood goals, and modeling the kind of interpersonal climate we think is desirable in an organization?

To summarize, the process-maintenance element is designed to accomplish several objectives: to model self-analysis and self-reflection as means of self-improvement; to model the action research principles of goal setting coupled with data feedback loops to guide and evaluate actions; to work to ensure ownership of the interventions and the entire program by organization members; to model the ability to detect and cope with problems and opportunities in the internal and the external environment; to test the effectiveness of interventions by utilizing feedback from the system; to test for relevancy of the program to the organization's needs; to test for timeliness of interventions; and to ensure that intended and unintended consequences do not obviate the organization's and the OD program's goals.

The importance of this component can hardly be overstated. Managing the OD process effectively can spell the difference between success and failure for the improvement effort. This component, maintenance and management of the OD process, may help to explain why there are many aborted OD efforts and few long-range, successful ones. The practicing-what-you-preach aspect probably contributes significantly to bringing about real, genotypic, lasting change in the organization instead of apparent, phenotypic, or "pasted on" change. In later chapters we pay considerable attention to the problems that can arise in OD programs as well as to issues and dimensions related to sound maintenance of the process.

We have identified three major components of an operational OD program as follows: the diagnostic component; the intervention, or action-taking, component; and the OD process-maintenance component. These components reflect the characteristics and foundations of the OD process discussed in the next chapter, and, in fact, the characteristics may be viewed as having determined to a great extent the *forms and functions* that operationally define organization development.

5

the nature of organization development
Characteristics and Foundations
of the OD Process

Examining the basic components of an OD program in operation afforded one look at the nature of organization development. In this chapter OD is examined from additional perspectives—call them underlying characteristics, distinguishing features, foundations, or theoretical and practice underpinnings.

OD can be characterized in several different ways—as a process, as a form of applied behavioral science, as normative change, as incorporating a systems approach to organizations, as similar to and based on an action research (data-based) model, as an experience-based learning mode, as emphasizing goals and objectives, and as concentrating on intact work teams as the primary instruments for organization improvement. Each of these facets adds something new to the picture of the OD process. Although several of these attributes were introduced in Chapter 2, we want to elaborate on them here.

OD IS AN ONGOING INTERACTIVE PROCESS

One understands much about the nature of OD by viewing it as an ongoing interactive process. A process is an identifiable flow of interrelated events moving over time toward some goal or end.[1] In the OD process, the identifiable flow of interrelated events consists of interventions in the client system and responses to the interventions. Behind the pattern is the overall OD strategy directing the selection, timing, and sequencing of in-

---

[1] Wendell French, *The Personnel Management Process,* 2nd ed. (Boston: Houghton Mifflin Company, 1970), p. 33.

tervention activities; this strategy ties the individual events together into a coherent, directioned thrust. In practice, an initial strategy will be formulated, and this will be modified and changed as events and experience suggest emergent directions and emergent problems.

But the essential point in calling OD a process is to characterize it as a dynamic, moving, changing thing. People learn new skills and forget old ones; the structure of the organization changes, and then another change is put on top of that; problems are solved and new ones develop; a sick subsystem gets well and a heretofore healthy one develops bad symptoms. There are good days and bad days for the OD program as well as successes and failures.

Another facet of OD as a process is that the process of improving organizations may be a process of "becoming"—of approaching some end state, a point-at-able condition, without ever reaching it in the usual sense of "arriving." Although most people would generally agree about whether one organization is "better" or "worse" than another in terms of organizational effectiveness, there is less agreement on when an organization has "arrived" and lack of agreement on the indicators used to signal that arrival. This is not to say that OD practitioners do not know where they are going and what they are trying to achieve, because that is not so; but it is to say that at this stage in the art and the science of organization development projections about the goals of the OD effort serve primarily as guides or heuristic servomechanisms rather than as definitive descriptions of an end state.

The ongoing process nature of OD implies that it is not to be regarded as a one-shot solution to organizational problems, but more as a "growing toward" greater effectiveness. Managing and directing the change of an organization's culture does not happen overnight; a more accurate time estimate is several years. Differing estimates of how long the process does take versus how long it should take may lead to problems between practitioners and organization members in that members may want and expect immediate results and may get discouraged when they are not forthcoming. On the other hand, a trap practitioners can get themselves into is to raise members' expectations, either deliberately or inadvertently, for quick answers to problems and then not be able to produce results. At the other end of the spectrum, the practitioner may emphasize the long-term nature of OD to the point that he frightens away a prospective client who has had little experience with the concept and feels he may be trapped into a several years' program that he does not like. Successful OD efforts can start with small beginnings and without long-range commitments, providing expectations are realistic.

The interactive nature of the process also implies a series of actions and reactions, initiated activities and the responses to these activities.

Organizational behavior is incredibly complex, and probably the only adequate way to conceptualize it is through an interaction theory of social behavior. But as Bennis, Schein, Berlew, and Steele indicate, we have no such theory in the social sciences at this time.[2] Viewing the OD process as a complex series of interactions promotes a better understanding of organizational dynamics, even though no comprehensive theory exists to help explain the phenomena. The interactive nature of the OD process, however, does suggest the necessity for effective feedback loops for monitoring the reactions to interventions, the readiness of subsystems for change, and emergent problems and new directions.

OD IS A FORM OF APPLIED BEHAVIORAL SCIENCE

An OD program applies the scientific and practice principles from several behavioral sciences: social psychology, social anthropology, sociology, psychiatry, economics, and political science. The OD practitioner is neither magician nor charlatan; he is simply translating what is known about people and organizations as found in behavioral science knowledge into applicable programs of actions. In fact, this section could be titled "demythologizing organization development" because we wish to show that OD is not a mysterious and magical spell cast upon an organization by the incantations of a behavioral scientist "change agent." Quite to the contrary, practitioners base their diagnoses and actions on the known, lawful-patterned events and dynamics that help explain individual, group, and organization behavior. Knowledge of these lawful patterns comes primarily from personality theory, social psychology, group dynamics, and organization theory, typically coupled with knowledge about theory and practice regarding adult education, planned change, systems theory, and a dash of operations research. Another definition of OD could be "OD is the application of behavioral knowledge, practices, and skills in ongoing systems in collaboration with system members."

A conventional distinction is usually made between (*a*) "pure" or basic science, the object of which is knowledge for its own sake, and (*b*) "technology," applied science, or practice, the object of which is knowledge to solve practical, pressing problems.[3] Greenwood discusses the activities of the practitioner as follows: "The problem that confronts a practitioner is customarily a state of disequilibrium that requires rectifica-

---

[2] W. G. Bennis, E. H. Schein, D. E. Berlew, and F. I. Steele, *Interpersonal Dynamics* (Homewood, Ill.: The Dorsey Press, 1964), pp. 2–3.

[3] Robert K. Merton and Daniel Lerner, "Social Scientists and Research Policy," in W. G. Bennis, K. D. Benne, and R. Chin, *The Planning of Change* (New York: Holt, Rinehart & Winston, Inc., 1961), pp. 53–69.

tion. The practitioner examines the problem situation, on the basis of which he prescribes a solution, that, hopefully, reestablishes the equilibrium, thereby solving the problem. This process is customarily referred to as diagnosis and treatment." [4] Both diagnosis and treatment consist of observing a situation, and on the basis of selected variables, placing it in a classification scheme or typology. The diagnostic typology allows the practitioner to know what category of situation he has examined; the treatment typology allows the practitioner to know what remedial efforts to apply to correct the problem. On this point, Greenwood states:

> The diagnostic and treatment typologies are employed together. Each type description of the diagnostic typology contains implications for a certain type of treatment. The practitioner uses treatment as the empirical test of his diagnosis, success corroborating the diagnosis, failure negating it and thus requiring rediagnosis. The principles of diagnosis and of treatment constitute the principles of practice, i.e., with their elaborations and implications constitute practice theory.[5]

It is from this "practice theory" that the OD practitioner works: first diagnosing the situation, then selecting and implementing treatments based on the diagnosis, and finally evaluating the effects of the treatments.

Organization development is both a result of applied behavioral science and a form of applied behavioral science; perhaps more accurately, it is a program of applying behavioral science to organizations. Figure 5-1 shows some of the inputs to applied behavioral science. The two bottom inputs, behavioral science research and behavioral science theory, are intended to represent contributions from "pure" or basic science; the two top inputs, practice research and practice theory, are intended to represent contributions from "applied" science.

Some examples of contributions from these four sources that are relevant for applying behavioral science in organization development are the following:

> Contributions from behavioral science theory:
> The importance of social norms in determining perceptions, motivations, and behaviors (Sherif)
> The role of an *exchange theory* of behavior that postulates that people tend to exchange approximately equivalent units to maintain a balance between what is given and received (Gouldner, Homans)
> The importance of the existing total field of forces in determining and predicting behavior (Lewin)

---

[4] Ernest Greenwood, "The Practice of Science and the Science of Practice" in Bennis, Benne, and Chin, *The Planning of Change*, p. 78.
[5] *Ibid.*, p. 79.

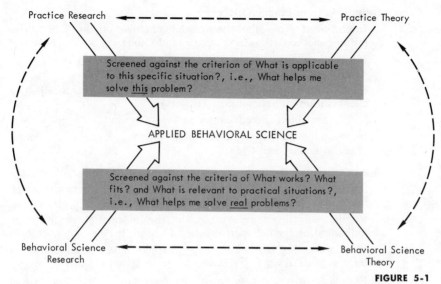

FIGURE 5-1

COMPOSITION OF APPLIED BEHAVIORAL SCIENCE

The relevance of role theory in accounting for stability and change in behavior (G. H. Mead)

The role and importance of *activities, interactions,* and *sentiments* as explanatory concepts for elementary social behavior (Homans)

The possibilities inherent in views of motivation different from those provided by older theories (McGregor, Herzberg, Maslow)

The place of learning theories, effects of reward and punishment, attitude change theories, etc.

Contributions from behavioral science research:

Studies on the causes, conditions, and consequences of induced competition on behavior within and between groups (Sherif, and Blake and Mouton)

Results on the effects of cooperative and competitive group goal structures on behavior within groups (Deutsch)

Studies on the effects of organizational and managerial climate on leadership style (Fleishman)

Studies on the variables relevant for organizational health (Likert)

Studies showing the importance of the social system in relation to the technical system (Trist and Bamforth)

Results from studies on different communication networks (Leavitt), causes and consequences of conformity (Asch), group problem solving (Kelley and Thibaut), and group dynamics (Cartwright and Zander)

Contributions from practice theory:

Implications from the theory and practice of the laboratory-training method (Bradford, Benne, and Gibb)

Implications from theories of group development (Schutz, and Bennis and Shepard)

New dimensions in the helping relationship and specifically the client-consultant relationship (Rogers)

New ideas about the education process (Dewey)

Implications and applications from theories of *planned change* (Bennis, Benne, and Chin).

Contributions from practice research:

Studies showing that feeding back survey research data can bring about organization change (Mann, Baumgartel)

Results indicating the importance of the informal work group on individual and group performance (Roethlisberger and Dickson)

Results showing the efficacy of grid organization development in large organizations (Blake, Mouton, Barnes, and Greiner)

Results showing the complexity of intraorganizational communication and interaction patterns on job performance (Whyte)

Results from the action research studies in Chapter 8 show important inputs from practice settings.[6]

These contributions are not meant to be exhaustive, but only to show some of the sources and kinds of information/knowledge that OD practitioners, as applied behavioral scientists, bring to the organizational setting.

OD IS A NORMATIVE–RE-EDUCATIVE STRATEGY OF CHANGING

Since organization development is a process for improving organizational effectiveness, this implies doing things differently and better, and this means changing some features of the organization (usually its processes and culture). To some people, change is a defense-provoking word; to others, change is a panacea for all problems. We agree with neither of these views. Instead we subscribe to the belief that change, when it is desired by the people who will be affected, and when it opens up alternatives of action rather than closing off alternatives, and when it seems to incorporate choices of action that in other situations have been demonstrated to be good ones or that by generally enlightened criteria (say, for example, the scientific method) are considered good ones—then

[6] See bibliography at the end of the chapter for references to the contributions of each of the above authors.

we believe that change is indicated as a desirable action step. OD is not a broadside attack on the values held by individuals, organizations, or a society, but it does represent a value framework, much of which will be discussed in the next chapter on assumptions and values in OD. For example, OD practitioners are not interested in changing people's values about religion, politics, marriage, the nation, and so forth; but they would try to change people's values in the direction of belief in the worth of the individual, belief in the dysfunctional aspects of many zero-sum games in the organization, belief that participation in decisions promotes feelings of self-worth, and the like. In addition, most OD practitioners would make known to clients their value systems and would permit the client to accept or reject them.

But organization development does involve change, and it rests on a particular strategy of changing that has implications for practitioners and organization members alike. Chin and Benne describe three types of strategies for changing.[7] First there are the empirical-rational strategies, based on the assumptions that men are rational, will follow their rational self-interest, and will change if and when they come to realize the change is advantageous to them. The second group of strategies are the normative–re-educative strategies, based on the assumptions that norms form the basis for behavior and change comes through a re-education process in which old norms are discarded and supplanted by new ones. The third set of strategies are the power-coercive strategies, based on the assumption that change is compliance of those with less power to the desires of those with more power. Evaluated against these three change approaches, OD is clearly seen to fall within the normative–re-educative category, although in some senses, it may represent a combination of the normative–re-educative with the empirical-rational. The nature of this second change strategy is indicated by Chin and Benne:

> A second group of strategies we call normative–re-educative. These strategies build upon assumptions about human motivation different from those underlying the first. The rationality and intelligence of men are not denied. Patterns of action and practice are supported by sociocultural norms and by commitments on the part of individuals to these norms. Sociocultural norms are supported by the attitude and value systems of individuals—normative outlooks which undergird their commitments. Change in a pattern of practice or action, according to this view, will occur only as the persons involved are brought to change their normative orientations to old patterns and develop commitments to new ones. And changes in normative orientations involve changes in

[7] R. Chin and K. Benne, "General Strategies for Effecting Changes in Human Systems," in W. G. Bennis, K. D. Benne, and R. Chin, *The Planning of Change,* 2nd ed. (New York: Holt, Rinehart & Winston, Inc., 1969), pp. 32–59.

attitudes, values, skills, and significant relationships, not just changes in knowledge, information, or intellectual rationales for action and practice.[8]

An illustration may clarify these three strategies of changing. Say the Salk polio vaccine has just been invented, tested, and cleared for public use, and you are in charge of disseminating it to the public. Your procedure would depend upon which strategy of changing you believed in. If you espoused the empirical-rational theory of changing, then you would assume that all rational, self-interested people (and that is everyone, just about) would use the vaccine if only they had information and knowledge about its availability and its efficacy. Your program, therefore, would be to disseminate the knowledge and information. As a consequence, everyone would take the vaccine, since it would be in his best interests.

On the other hand, if you held a normative–re-educative belief about changing, you would do additional things. While you would not disbelieve or disregard man's intelligence, rationality, and self-interest, you would also believe that some of his behavior was rooted in socio-cultural norms, values, and beliefs that must be changed in order for him to accept and use the vaccine. Some of these beliefs might be that "all new drugs are dangerous until they have been on the market for ten years"; "My neighbor, Mrs. Jones, isn't going to use the vaccine, and neither am I since she's always right about these things"; "Well, no one in my family has ever had polio, so I'm not afraid of getting it and don't need to be vaccinated." Holding to the second strategy of changing, you would assume that norms and values had to be changed, in addition to making the information available to the public. You would mount both an education campaign about the new drug and a re-education campaign to change some norms and values.

If you held to a power-coercive strategy of changing, your task would be straightforward: you would pass a law stating all persons must get vaccinated, and you would ensure and enforce compliance to the law. If you had the power to pass the law, and power to enforce the law, the people would take the vaccine.

The point here is that there are different strategies for effecting change, and OD is based primarily on a normative–re-educative one and secondarily on a rational-empirical one. Focusing on the normative–re-educative strategy for change, as practiced in an organization development program, the following implications are associated with that change strategy: the *client* defines what changes and improvements he wants to make, rather than the change agent; the change agent attempts to intervene

[8] *Ibid.*, p. 34.

in a mutual, collaborative way with the client as they together define problems and seek solutions; anything hindering effective problem solving is brought to light and publicly examined, that is doubts, anxieties, and negative feelings are surfaced for "working through"; the methods and knowledge of the behavioral sciences are used as resources by both change agents and clients; and solutions to problems are not a priori assigned to greater technical information or knowledge but may reside in values, attitudes, relationships, and customary ways of doing things.[9] The desire for and the form of re-education are decisions for the client to make; implementing the re-education chosen by the client is the work of the practitioner. These are far-reaching implications for OD for several reasons: they significantly dictate practitioner values and behaviors; they give the clients considerable choice and control over the situation; they impel a collaborative effort rather than a "doing something to" effort; and they lead to more options and alternatives rather than fewer ones for both the client and the practitioner.

Our definition of organization development refers to improving and managing the organization's culture—a clear reference to the normative nature of the change process. Burke and Hornstein emphasize the normative nature of OD even more in their definition: "Organization development is a process of planned change. It involves change of an organization's culture from one which avoids an examination of social processes in organizations, especially decision making, planning and communications, to one which institutionalizes and legitimizes this examination." [10] These authors assert that the initial focus of OD is normative change and that individual change is merely a by-product. The nature of the change in the culture indicated by Burke and Hornstein is congruent with our definition and with those of others. These changes are not of the nature to affront, belittle, coerce, or harass individuals' personally held, deep-seated values but relate more to norms, attitudes, and values about how to get the organizational mission accomplished.

Warren Bennis, in a discussion on the characteristics of organization development, comments on the normative aspect of this process as follows:

> change agents share a set of *normative goals* based on their philosophy.
> ... Most commonly sought are:
> 1. Improvement in interpersonal competence.
> 2. A shift in values so that human factors and feelings come to be considered legitimate.
> 3. Development of increased understanding between and within working groups in order to reduce tensions.

[9] Based on a discussion in Chin and Benne, *ibid.,* pp. 44–45.
[10] W. W. Burke and H. A. Hornstein "Introduction to the Social Technology of Organization Development," prepublication copy, 1971, p. 1.

4. Development of more effective "team management," i.e., the capacity . . . for functional groups to work more competently.
5. Development of better methods of "conflict resolution." Rather than the usual bureaucratic methods which rely mainly on suppression, compromise, and unprincipled power, more rational and open methods of conflict resolution are sought.
6. Development of organic rather than mechanical systems. This is a strong reaction against the idea of organizations as mechanism which managers "work on," like pushing buttons.[11]

Bennis likewise emphasizes the educational nature of OD: "Organization development (OD) is a response to change, a complex educational strategy intended to change the beliefs, attitudes, values, and structure of organizations so that they can better adapt to new technologies, markets, and challenges, and the dizzying rate of change itself." [12]

Although a normative–re-educative strategy of changing is most characteristic of the OD process, there is a rational-empirical aspect to it also. Many of the objectives of OD interventions have an appeal as being "obviously" a better way. For example, it is often intrinsically satisfying to learn to manage conflict well, or to learn to make better decisions, or to learn to manage against clearly defined objectives. Clients often know there must be better ways of doing things and have the strong desire to identify these better ways, but they have never been presented with the information and knowledge. Once given the knowledge, there is immediate changeover to new ways of managing and new ways of behaving. From our experience, much change does occur in organization development through the processes described in the rational-empirical strategy for changing.

OD VIEWS ORGANIZATIONS FROM A SYSTEMS APPROACH

Systems concepts relevant to organization development are discussed in Chapter 7, so we will touch on them only briefly here. A systems approach views and emphasizes organizational phenomena and dynamics in their interrelatedness, their connectedness, their interdependence, and their interaction. This is the perspective we believe is useful for understanding organizational life. As Chin says of the systems approach: "The analytic model of system demands that we treat the phenomena and the concepts for organizing the phenomena as if there existed organization,

---

[11] Warren Bennis, *Organization Development: Its Nature, Origins, and Prospects* (Reading, Mass.: Addison-Wesley Publishing Company, 1969), p. 15.
[12] *Ibid.,* p. 2.

interaction, interdependency, and integration of parts and elements. System analysis assumes structure and stability within some arbitrarily sliced and frozen time period." [13]

Several consequences of viewing organizations from this perspective have value and functionality for applying behavioral science to organization development.

First, issues, events, forces, and incidents are not viewed as isolated phenomena; they occur in relation to other events, issues, phenomena. Understanding only the phenomenon and not understanding it in relation to other phenomena is to have only a half understanding.

Second, a systems approach encourages analysis of events in terms of multiple causation rather than single causation. The real world is complex; events in it are complex. It is probably a more accurate description of reality to posit multiple causes to events; this is facilitated by the systems approach.

Third, and this is taken from Kurt Lewin's field theory in social psychology, the field of forces at the time of the event are the relevant forces for analysis.[14] This dictum moves the practitioner away from an analysis of historical events and forces to an examination of the contemporary events and forces—to a more existential vantage point.

Fourth, one cannot change one part of a system without influencing other parts in some ways. A related point to this one is that the systems viewpoint inclines the practitioner to anticipate multiple effects rather than single effects. These effects show up in other parts of the system and also in "surprises" in the part of the system with which he is working. Anticipating multiple causes and multiple effects, a viewpoint practiced by OD practitioners, does take many of the surprises out of organizational dynamics.

The fifth and final point is that if one wants to change a system, he changes the system, not just its component parts. Organization development is the development of a system, not only of the parts of a system. Blake and Mouton address this issue:

Organization development means development of the organization. Because of the history of education, training and development in industry, the inclination on seeing the word organization before development is to think and substitute for it the word individual. If the reader does this, he will miss the deeper implication of what is presented. The reason is that he will fail to comprehend how deeply the culture of a corporation controls the behavior of all of its individuals. While the ultimate objec-

[13] Robert Chin, "The Utility of System Models and Developmental Models for Practitioners," in Bennis, Benne, and Chin, *The Planning of Change*, 2nd ed., pp. 299–300.

[14] Kurt Lewin, *Field Theory in Social Science* (New York: Harper & Bros., 1951).

tive of organization development is to liberate all of the individuals within it, so that they will be free, participative, and contributive to problem solving, in order to achieve corporate purposes of profitability, this objective cannot be reached until the constraints that operate within the corporation's culture have been studied and deliberately rejected. The key difference between individual and organization development will be found in this proposition.[15]

Additional systems concepts are presented later in the book, but one of the foundations for organization development is a systems approach. When practitioners started viewing organizations from a systems approach, a significant step toward the realization of organization development was taken.

OD IS A DATA-BASED APPROACH TO PLANNED CHANGE

A data-based model, the action research model, underlies sound OD programs and is a significant facet of the nature of organization development. The action research model is discussed in Chapter 8, but we want to make a few comments here. Many OD interventions are designed either to generate data or to plan actions based on data. A key value inculcated in organization members is a belief in the validity, desirability, and usefulness of *data about the system itself*, specifically, data about the system's culture and processes.

The data-based nature of organization development has some features that distinguish it from other data-based change activities. Some of the characteristics and their implications are the following. First, strong emphasis is placed on the value of data in the OD process, perhaps stronger than that in most change programs. As a consequence of this, organization members learn how to collect, work with, and utilize data for problem solving in the organization. Second, in OD programs, specific kinds of data are preferred over others. For example, data about the organization's human and social processes would be used more than technical data, financial data, market information, and the like. Third, in OD programs, the data usually "belong to" and are used by the people who generated them. This means that an attitude survey, for example, is not conducted just so that top management can study the results; rather it is conducted so that the contributors at all levels may have an

[15] R. R. Blake and J. S. Mouton, *Building a Dynamic Corporation through Grid Organization Development* (Reading, Mass.: Addison-Wesley Publishing Company, 1969), p. vi.

accurate picture of the situations they confront and may then plan action programs to capitalize on the positive attributes and eradicate the negative attributes. The data are public; the data are the property of all organization members; the data are a springboard to action. Fourth, the contradictory data or the discrepancy data are viewed as "nuggets" rather than as nuisances in OD programs. They point the way to differences in preceptions, motivations, attitudes, and so forth, that often, once discovered, can lead to breakthroughs in improving the organization's effectiveness. For example, if one hierarchical level views the compensation plan as fair and equitable and another level views it as unjust and unfair (and if neither of these levels knew the other felt that way), then the finding of this nugget can point toward action plans to decide what to do about the discrepancy. Fifth, in OD programs, feelings toward "facts" tend to shift from viewing facts as either "good" or "bad" to looking at the consequences or functionality/dysfunctionality of the facts. For example, a particular leadership style, highly authoritarian, may be a fact. The important thing about this fact is not to label it as good or bad, but to understand the consequences of manifesting this leadership style, and to understand the conditions under which it is functional (for certain results) and dysfunctional for other results. This is, then, a shift from *evaluating* data to *describing* data—a subtle but important difference. When data are described, people tend to become less defensive about them, compared to when they are evaluated. A sixth point is that in OD programs data tend to be used as aids to problem solving rather than as "clubs" to enforce certain behaviors. One of the goals of organization development is to build the climate in the system to the point where data are used not to punish people but to aid them in problem solving. Seventh, the strong data base used in organization development is similar to that of the scientific method, in the sense that decisions are made increasingly on the basis of empirical facts rather than power, position, tradition, persuasion, and so forth. As a final note, the data used in the OD process stem from the stated needs and problems of the system members, that is, they are data to supply answers to central needs of the organization and its members.

OD IS EXPERIENCE-BASED

The experience-based nature of the OD process derives from an underlying belief of most OD practitioners that people learn how to do things by doing them. And they learn about organizational dynamics by experiencing them and reflecting on the experience. These beliefs are based on tenets of the laboratory training movement. People learn about the need to manage conflict when they experience the deleterious effects of conflict; people learn to make decisions by making some and then evaluating them. When people are engaged in real experiences, they are engaged with their minds, emotions, strivings—their whole beings. There are no artificial separations engendered, say, by memorizing something so that at some future time one may act in a certain way.

Instead of treating hypothetical problems and abstract organizational issues, OD interventions tend to focus on the real behavior of individuals and groups, tend to try to solve real problems, and tend to derive generalizations about organizational dynamics inductively from experience. Then more general theory input, knowledge building, and skill building are overlaid on the experience base as needed.

Experience-based learning calls not just for exposure to an experience but also for reflection about the experience. Organizational members experience something through an activity, then reflect on that experience to derive learnings and generalizations about the phenomenon. Many OD interventions call for scheduling reflection time after an activity, during which the participants examine such issues as the following: What were the causal relationships we found in this activity? What were the things we appeared to do right in this task? What things hindered our reaching our goals? What can we learn from this experience that may apply to future experiences and tasks? This constant questioning and reflecting is itself related to the goal of increasing people's ability to "learn how to learn." Essentially the concept of learning how to learn refers to having an inquiry/experimental attitude "set" that the individual takes into all his experiences; he continually examines his own experiences in order that he may learn and change and grow.

Many OD practitioners have also worked extensively with laboratory training methods and procedures. The lab-training approach to learning is heavily dependent upon experiential learning—learning about something by experiencing it and then reflecting on the experience. Experiential learning methods appear to be particularly efficacious for learning about human and social relations, that is, increasing interpersonal skills, learning about small group dynamics, and so forth. When experiential methods were applied to other task areas, such as planning, goal setting, and decision making, they were found to be equally potent for learning. Various kinds of experiential learning exercises are used in organization development, and this experience-based component is thus another cornerstone in the foundation.

OD EMPHASIZES GOAL SETTING AND PLANNING

It has been said before, but we want to say again, that goal setting and planning are important features of the OD process. The OD process has goals, specifically those of improving, in various ways, the functioning of the organization. One of the ways OD programs facilitate organizational improvement is through emphasizing the importance of goals and plans, structuring learning activities designed to improve goal-setting and planning skills. Beckhard addresses this issue as follows: "One of the major assumptions underlying organization-development efforts and much managerial strategy today is the need to assure that organizations are managing against goals. Healthy organizations tend to have goal-setting at all levels." [16]

Both organizations and individuals need to manage their affairs against goals—explicit, measurable, obtainable goals. To help achieve this for the organization, OD interventions may be directed toward examination of the planning function, strategy-making processes, and goal-setting processes at the individual group, and organizational levels. To help achieve this for the individual, OD interventions are directed toward the activities just mentioned and may also devote time to a series of activities called "life- and career-planning" exercises. Career development and life-planning activities are those in which individuals work on clarifying their life and career objectives and goals and determine how they can achieve them. In addition, when management by objectives is a part of an OD program, work teams with their immediate superiors learn to set realistic objectives which will be periodically reviewed. In this way individuals develop goal-setting abilities.

The importance of goal setting in OD programs, at both the individual and the organizational levels, probably represents a response to changes in the culture of organizations in this country in the last decade or two. It used to be that goal setting and planning were the sole function of the top echelons of the organization, while the functions of the lower echelons were to carry out the plans and help reach the objectives. It is now believed that wider participation in goal setting leads to a greater utilization of an organization's resources, human and technical, and results in significantly better plans. In addition, the plans that have been the contribution of many people at all levels of the organization probably have more chance of being realistic and attainable and also have some built-in support for carrying them out. But individuals and groups at

---

[16] Richard Beckhard, *Organization Development: Strategies and Models* (Reading, Mass.: Addison-Wesley Publishing Company, 1969), p. 35.

lower organizational levels often did not have the skills necessary to do good plan making, since they had never been called upon to do so. OD interventions directed toward learning and practicing these skills attempt to meet this need of the organization and its members.

The Blake and Mouton *grid organization development model* is particularly relevant for teaching goal-setting and planning abilities. In this six-phase model, Phase 4 consists of the top management team studying the properties of an "ideal strategic corporate model"—what properties a corporation should optimally possess if it is to maximize its goals. This is followed by analyzing the organization to see where it falls short of the ideal model. Phase 5 consists of developing implementation tactics for converting the organization from what it is and has been to what it should become as an ideal corporation. The paradigm first teaches the characteristics and properties of a desirable ideal organization, then measures the real organization against that ideal, then develops implementation procedures for moving from "what we are now" to "what we want to be." [17]

The goal-setting and planning interventions concentrate on the following major skills and abilities: (1) learning to set goals and objectives, (2) learning to translate goals into actions and procedures for achieving them, and (3) learning how to plan and make decisions to facilitate goal attainment. (In a sense, this third point is a restatement of the first two points.) What we mean by goals and plans can best be shown by calling on writings from the fields of management and administration. Koontz and O'Donnell describe the planning function as follows:

> Plans involve selecting enterprise objectives and departmental plans and programs, and determining ways of reaching them. Plans thus provide a rational approach to preselected objectives. . . . Planning is deciding in advance what to do, how to do it, when to do it, and who is to do it. . . . Planning is an intellectual process, the conscious determination of courses of action, the basing of decisions on purpose, facts, and considered estimates.[18]

The relation of planning and goals is suggested by Kast and Rosenzweig as follows:

> Basically, goals are plans expressed as results to be achieved. In this broad sense, goals include objectives, purposes, missions, deadlines, standards, target, quotas, etc. Goals represent not only the end point of

---

[17] Blake and Mouton, *Building a Dynamic Corporation*, p. 16.
[18] Harold Koontz and Cyril O'Donnell, *Principles of Management*, 4th ed. (New York: McGraw-Hill Book Company, 1968), p. 81.

planning but the end toward which the other managerial activities, such as organizing and controlling, are aimed.[19]

Thus, the emphasis on goal setting and planning in the OD process began as a response to the needs of organizations to have these skills available to all levels of the organization. Now the importance of "managing against objectives" and its positive consequences for better effectiveness are recognized as important in their own right. It is this belief that makes this feature another of the foundations of organization development.

OD ACTIVITIES FOCUS ON INTACT WORK TEAMS

A fundamental belief in organization development is that the organization does its work through work teams of a variety of kinds and natures. A second fundamental belief is that changing the culture, processes, relationships, and ways of performing tasks within these teams is a way to achieve permanent and lasting improvement in the organization. From a historical point of view, it was probably a realization of these two beliefs and the actions on them taken by Blake, Mouton, Shepard, Horowitz, McGregor, and others that gave birth to what we now know as organization development. The capacity for learning and change that comes from working with intact organizational teams can never be captured by the more traditional "stranger-type" learning activities.`

Many different kinds of teams have salience and significance for the organizational members and for the OD practitioners. The potency and ability to make things happen by intact work teams working together to improve their team effectiveness is frankly astounding compared with working with a group of individuals who are organizationally irrelevant to each other. This is true for a number of reasons, some of which are the following. First, much individual behavior is rooted in the socio-cultural norms and values of the work team. If the team, as a team, changes those norms and values, the effect on individual behavior is immediate and lasting. Second, the intact work team possesses the "reality configuration of relationships" that the individuals must in fact accommodate to and learn to utilize and cope with. This is to say that many of the "significant others" of the individual's work world are in the work group. Effective (or ineffective) relationships with these people can have far-reaching effects on the individual's performance and behavior. Third, the "reality configuration of organizational dynamics" that the indi-

[19] Fremont E. Kast and James E. Rosenzweig, *Organization and Management* (New York: McGraw-Hill Book Company, 1970), p. 439.

viduals must accommodate to are found in the work team. By this we mean that the work team is the source of most of the individual's knowledge about organizational processes such as communications, decision making, and goal setting. These are the processes that most influence the individual's behavior. Fourth, it is commonly believed that many of the individual's needs for social interaction, status, recognition, and respect are satisfied by his work group, consisting of both peers and superior. Any process that improves the work team's processes or task performance will thus probably be related to central needs of the individual members.

In our experience, most OD programs rely heavily on interventions designed to improve work team relationships, processes, and task performance. In the Grid approach to organization development, for example, Phase 1 concentrates on learnings about managerial style and interpersonal competence for individual managers; then Phase 2 moves immediately into improving the work team culture and processes through activities in intact work teams.[20]

While working with intact groups to improve their functioning can be a powerful instrumentality for organizational change, it can also do considerable damage to the team if the activities are poorly conceived or poorly executed. Because the work team is so important to the individual, doing anything to destroy the relationships or to impair the processes or the ability for task performance can cause a profound and disastrous effect. This is another reason why we believe that an external change agent should be involved in the early stages of an OD program. There are numerous tales within the OD trade of calamitous effects in team-building sessions—some of these are true, but many of them are mythical. Team sessions are complex affairs, and a professional should be present to insure that they go right.

SUMMARY

In this chapter we have continued to present our conception of the nature of organization development. OD as an operational process was seen to possess three basic components: the diagnostic, the action (or intervention), and the process-maintenance components, although we said that, in effect, all these components are interventions into the client system. In this chapter the foundations or building blocks characterizing the OD process have been explicated. Organization development was seen to have the following characteristics: it is an ongoing process; it is a form of applied behavioral science; it constitutes a normative–re-educative

---

[20] Blake and Mouton, *Building a Dynamic Corporation,* p. 16.

strategy for changing; it utilizes a systems approach; it is a data-based problem-solving model; it reflects an experience-based learning model; it emphasizes goal setting and the planning function; and it involves intact work teams.

These foundations suggest an important conclusion: OD is the confluence of several diverse streams, all of which define the organization development process. OD is not one or two of these, but the result of all of these. Organization development represents the process emerging from the coming together at this point in time of the foundations—and each of these foundations was itself the result of diverse streams from earlier theories and earlier practices.

BIBLIOGRAPHY

ASCH, S., "Studies of Independence and Conformity: A Minority of One against a Unanimous Majority," *Psychological Monograph,* 70, No. 9 (1956).

BAUMGARTEL, H., "Using Employee Questionnaire Results for Improving Organizations: The Survey 'Feedback' Experiment,"—*Kansas Business Review,* 12 (December 1959), 2–6.

BENNIS, W. G., K. D. BENNE, and R. CHIN, *The Planning of Change.* New York: Holt, Rinehart & Winston, Inc., 1961.

BENNIS, W. G., and H. A. SHEPARD, "A Theory of Group Development," *Human Relations,* 9, No. 4 (1956), 415–38.

BLAKE, R. R., and J. S. MOUTON, "Conformity, Resistance, and Conversion," in I. A. Berg and B. M. Bass, eds., *Conformity and Deviation,* pp. 1–37. New York: Harper & Row, Publishers, 1961.

BLAKE, R. R., J. S. MOUTON, L. B. BARNES, and L. E. GREINER, "Breakthrough in Organization Development," *Harvard Business Review,* 42 (November–December 1964), 133–55.

BRADFORD, L. P., J. R. GIBB, and K. D. BENNE, eds., *T-Group Theory and Laboratory Method.* New York: John Wiley & Sons, Inc., 1964.

CARTWRIGHT, D., and A. ZANDER, *Group Dynamics* (2nd ed.). New York: Harper & Row, Publishers, 1960.

DEUTSCH, M., "A Theory of Cooperation and Competition," *Human Relations,* 2, No. 2 (1949), 129–52.

DEWEY, J., *How We Think* (rev. ed.). New York: D. C. Heath & Company, 1933.

FLEISHMAN, E. A., "Leadership Climate, Human Relations Training and Supervisory Behavior," *Personnel Psychology,* 6 (Summer 1953), 205–22.

GOULDNER, A. W., "The Norm of Reciprocity: A Preliminary Statement," *American Sociological Review,* 25 (April 1960), 161–78.

HERZBERG, F., B. MAUSNER, and B. SNYDERMAN, *The Motivation to Work.* New York: John Wiley & Sons, Inc., 1959.

HOMANS, G. C., *The Human Group.* New York: Harcourt, Brace & World, Inc., 1950.

————, *Social Behavior: Its Elementary Forms.* New York: Harcourt, Brace & World, Inc., 1961.

KELLEY, H. H., and J. W. THIBAUT, "Group Problem Solving," in G. Lindzey and E. Aronson, eds., *Handbook of Social Psychology* (2nd ed.), IV, 1–101. Reading, Mass.: Addison-Wesley Publishing Company, 1969.

LEAVITT, H. J., "Some Effects of Certain Communication Patterns on Group Performance," *Journal of Abnormal and Social Psychology,* 46 (January 1951), 38–50.

LEWIN, K., *Field Theory in Social Science.* New York: Harper & Bros., Publishers, 1951.

LIKERT, R., *New Patterns of Management.* New York: McGraw-Hill Book Company, 1961.

McGREGOR, D. M., *The Human Side of Enterprise.* New York: McGraw-Hill Book Company, 1960.

MANN, F. C., "Studying and Creating Change," in W. G. Bennis, K. D. Benne, and R. Chin, *The Planning of Change,* pp. 605–13. New York: Holt, Rinehart, & Winston, Inc., 1961.

MASLOW, A., *Motivation and Personality.* New York: Harper & Row, Publishers, 1964.

MEAD, G. H., *Mind, Self and Society.* Chicago: University of Chicago Press, 1934.

ROETHLISBERGER, F. J., and W. J. DICKSON, *Management and the Worker.* Cambridge: Harvard University Press, 1956.

ROGERS, C. R., *Client-Centered Therapy.* Boston: Houghton Mifflin Company, 1951.

SCHUTZ, W., *FIRO: A Three-Dimensional Theory of Interpersonal Behavior.* New York: Holt, Rinehart & Winston, Inc., 1958.

SHERIF, M., *The Psychology of Social Norms.* New York: Harper & Bros., 1936.

————, O. J. HARVEY, B. J. WIIITE, W. R. HOOD, and C. SHERIF, *Intergroup Conflict and Cooperation: The Robbers Cave Experiment.* Norman, Oklahoma: University Book Exchange, 1961.

TRIST, E. L., and K. W. BAMFORTH, "Some Social and Psychological Consequences of the Longwall Method of Coal-Getting," *Human Relations,* 4, No. 1 (1951), 1–38.

WHYTE, W. F., *Human Relations in the Restaurant Industry.* New York: McGraw-Hill Book Company, 1948.

6

Underlying Assumptions
and Values

Implicit in the preceding chapters and throughout the book are a number of underlying assumptions and values we should now make explicit. These assumptions, basic to most organization development activities, relate to people as individuals, to people as group members and as leaders, and to people as members of total organizational systems. The following appear to be some of the basic assumptions of organization development efforts and, in general, are congruent with the theories of McGregor, Likert, Argyris, Bennis, Schein, Maslow, and Herzberg.[1]

ASSUMPTIONS ABOUT PEOPLE AS INDIVIDUALS

We think organization development efforts make two basic assumptions about people. One has to do with personal growth and the other with constructive contributions.

The first assumption about people is that most individuals have drives toward personal growth and development if provided an environ-

[1] See, for example, Douglas McGregor, *The Professional Manager* (New York: McGraw-Hill Book Company, 1967); Rensis Likert, *The Human Organization: Its Management and Value* (New York: McGraw-Hill Book Company, 1967); Chris Argyris, *Integrating the Individual and the Organization* (New York: John Wiley & Sons, Inc., 1964); Edgar H. Schein and Warren G. Bennis, *Personal and Organizational Change through Group Methods* (New York: John Wiley & Sons, Inc., 1965); Abraham Maslow, *Motivation and Personality,* 2nd ed. (New York: Harper & Row, Publishers, 1970); and Frederick Herzberg, *Work and the Nature of Man* (Cleveland: The World Publishing Company, 1966). This discussion has also been influenced by "Some Assumptions about Change in Organizations" in a reading notebook entitled *Program for Specialists in Organization Training and Development* (NTL Institute for Applied Behavioral Science, 1967) and by staff members who participated in that program.

ment that is both supportive and challenging. Most people want to become more of what they are capable of becoming.

The second assumption, related to the first, is that most people desire to make, and are capable of making, a higher level of contribution to the attainment of organizational goals than most organizational environments will permit. A tremendous amount of constructive energy can be tapped if organizations recognize this; for example, by asking for and acting on suggestions. Frequently, however, organizational members learn that what they perceive to be constructive efforts may be self-defeating in the sense that these efforts are not rewarded and may be penalized. For example, attempts at lateral communications between two departments to solve some problem may be throttled through adherence to some principle about the chain of command.

These assumptions differ markedly from more traditional views about people. As Tannenbaum and Davis state it:

> The traditional view of individuals is that they can be defined in terms of given interests, knowledge, skills and personality characteristics: they can gain new knowledge, acquire additional skills, and even at times change their interests, but it is rare that people really change. This view, when buttressed by related organizational attitudes and modes, insures a relative fixity of individuals, with crippling effects.[2]

Thus, one can view people as fixed entities, or one can view them as potentially "in process" or in "the process of becoming." [3] The latter assumption underlies many OD interventions—many of which are aimed at unleashing drives toward personal growth and contribution or are aimed at modifying organizational constraints that are having a dampening or throttling effect.

ASSUMPTIONS ABOUT PEOPLE IN GROUPS AND ABOUT LEADERSHIP

The importance of the work team has long been recognized, and the significance of the "informal" part of group life has received considerable attention since the Hawthorne studies of the late 1920s and early 1930s.[4] Extensive knowledge about group dynamics and collabo-

[2] Robert Tannenbaum and Sheldon Davis, "Values, Man and Organizations," *Industrial Management Review*, 10 (Winter 1969), 68–70.

[3] See Gordon W. Allport, *Becoming* (New Haven, Conn.: Yale University Press, 1955).

[4] For the major work growing out of these studies see F. J. Roethlisberger and William J. Dickson, *Management and the Worker* (Cambridge: Harvard University Press, 1956).

rative ways of managing group culture, however, has had a more recent origin. In particular, the laboratory-training movement of post–World War II has contributed to this knowledge. The following are some assumptions growing mainly out of this recent history.

The first assumption is that one of the most psychologically relevant reference groups for most people is the work group, including peers and the superior. What goes on in the work team, at the informal level in particular, has great significance for feelings of satisfaction and competence.

A related assumption is that most people wish to be accepted and to interact cooperatively with at least one small reference group, and usually with more than one group, that is, the work group, the family, and so forth. Furthermore, most people are capable of greatly increasing their effectiveness and of helping their reference groups solve problems. From our experience, most work groups have only begun to utilize their resources for effective collaboration. Stating the case negatively, a great deal of energy is expended *sub rosa* around such issues as inclusion-exclusion if there is no collaborative effort to examine and manage such dimensions.

A third assumption is that for a group to optimize its effectiveness, the formal leader cannot perform all the leadership and maintenance functions in all circumstances at all times, hence group members must assist each other with effective leadership and member behavior. For many managers and groups, these are difficult patterns from which to extricate themselves and frequently require a change in perspective on the part of both the manager and the total group. For example, if the manager begins to realize that improvements in unit functioning really require fuller participation on the part of all subordinates, the norms of the group may need to be examined to legitimate such participation. To illustrate—the current norms may call for deference to one or two more vocal members, or the norm may be to avoid issues facing the total unit in order to concentrate efforts on solving narrower problems where there is a more immediate payoff.

A fourth assumption is that suppressed feelings adversely affect problem solving, personal growth, and job satisfaction. The culture in most groups and organizations tends to suppress the expression of feelings that people have about each other and their behaviors—both positive and negative—about what they are doing and about where they and their organizations are heading. An emphasis on "rationality" seems to assume that emotions are best handled by repressing them—that feelings are taboo. This does not mean that the expression of feelings per se will be helpful or that, overnight, individuals and groups will have the skill to manage collaboratively the organizational underworld of sentiments. The development of such skill requires much learning and much of it together in the group that wishes to improve its performance. Viewing feelings as data important to the organization, however, coupled with the development of group skills in dealing with feelings, tends to open up many avenues for improved goal setting, leadership, communications, conflict resolution, problem solving, between-group collaboration, and morale.

A fifth assumption is that the level of interpersonal trust, support, and cooperation is much lower in most groups and organizations than is either necessary or desirable, in spite of drives toward these same qualities. Typically a number of forces contribute to such situations, including an absence of viewing feelings as important data, lack of group problem-solving skills, or reward and performance review systems that reinforce dysfunctional competition.

A sixth assumption about people in groups is that the solutions to most attitudinal and motivational problems in organizations are transactional. That is, such problems have the greatest chance of constructive solution if all parties in the system or subsystem alter their mutual relationships. The objective becomes, not how can A get B to perform, but *how can A and B work together to modify their interactions toward becoming more mutually effective.* Thus, the unit for attention becomes a system larger than one individual. This is not to deny the importance of the individual but to stress the significance of the interactional nature of human relationships in the organizational setting.

ASSUMPTIONS ABOUT PEOPLE IN ORGANIZATIONAL SYSTEMS

A number of ideas or assumptions about people in systems more complex than groups also underlie organization development efforts. Some of these assumptions follow, and others will be elaborated upon in Chapter 7.

In recent years it has frequently been observed that organizations tend to be characterized by overlapping work groups, with the superior and others serving, in Likert's terminology, as "linking pins." [5] (See Figure 6-1.[6]) Thus, a manager is a member of at least two work teams —as the superior in one and as a subordinate and peer in another. This leads to an assumption relevant to OD: the interrelated dynamics of both of these work teams and the manager's behavior in both work teams are

[5] See Rensis Likert, *New Patterns of Management* (New York: McGraw-Hill Book Company, 1961), p. 113.

[6] This figure is from Rensis Likert, *New Patterns of Management* (New York, McGraw-Hill Book Company, 1961), p. 133. Used with permission of McGraw-Hill Book Company.

highly significant factors in organizational life. To give only one example, the behavior of Manager Jones in meeting with his superior and his peers will tend to influence and be congruent with the way he runs meetings with his subordinates.

This notion of overlapping work groups is further complicated by the fact that it is common practice in many organizations to involve people in committees or task forces that draw members from several work groups. These can be viewed as temporary work teams which have a life of their own and which exist concurrently and in an overlapping way with the more "permanent" work teams.[7] The culture of these temporary work teams carries over into the culture of the more permanent work teams, and vice versa.

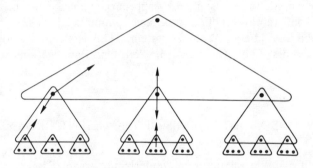

(The arrows indicate the linking pin function)

FIGURE 6-1

THE LINKING PIN FUNCTION

A second major assumption about people in organizations is that policies and practices of the broader organization affect the small work group and vice versa. Another way of saying this is that what happens to one subsystem (goal, social, structural, technological, task, or interface —for a description of these subsystems, see Chapter 7) will affect and

[7] Robert L. Kahn and others have elaborated on an "overlapping-role set" model which views people as occupying roles that are linked to others—subordinates, superiors, peers, and even to outsiders—in terms of interdependency or association. These other people are seen as constituting a "role set." One can then study behavior in terms of *role conflict,* when people in the role set differ in their expectations of the incumbent of the role, or in terms of role ambiguity, when role set makers do not communicate expectations to the role incumbent. For a summary of this model, see Edgar H. Schein, *Organizational Psychology* (Englewood Cliffs, N.J.: Prentice-Hall, Inc., 1965), pp. 94–95. For the original, see Robert L. Kahn *et al., Organizational Stress: Studies in Role Conflict and Ambiguity* (New York: John Wiley & Sons, Inc., 1964).

be influenced by other parts of the total system. It is obvious that personnel policies pertaining to hiring and wages, for example, can have a high impact on group attitudes. As another example, aggressive pressure for rights and privileges from one department can precipitate widespread perceptions of inequities or unfairness by people in other units, and ultimately a review of and changes in corporate personnel policies are likely to occur.

A third assumption about organizations is that "win-lose" conflict strategies between people and groups, in which one comes off the triumphant winner and the other the defensive loser, while realistic and appropriate in some situations, are not optimal in the long run to the solution of most organizational problems. Many problems can better be approached in terms of "how can we all win?"

Finally, improved performance stemming from organization development efforts needs to be sustained by appropriate changes in the appraisal, compensation, training, staffing, task, and communications subsystems—in short, in the total human resources system. (This is a complex topic which will be discussed in Chapter 15, "System Ramifications and New Demands.")

ASSUMPTIONS ABOUT VALUES OF THE CLIENT ORGANIZATION

Another basic assumption underlying organization development activities is that members of the system must, in general, place value in collaborative effort and in the constructive end products of the system, either current or potential. Some values must be held in common between protagonists if conflict-reducing and problem-solving techniques are to be useful; otherwise one or both tend to resort to raw power. To state the case negatively and to focus on some recent between-organization phenomena, organization development strategies will be unsuccessful to the degree that system members place value in anarchy, hate, violence, or destruction. This is not to say that organization development has no role in the management of dissent—it can have, but power becomes an overriding factor when values become highly polarized.

A further, and related, basic assumption underlying organization development activities is that value is placed on the welfare of all system members, particularly by the people having the most power over others. This assumption is the most basic and perhaps the most obvious one of all, but it needs to be made explicit. Both assumptions about the values of the client system need to be tested early in any organization development efforts, and any serious incongruities worked out between consultant and client, or the relationship should be terminated.

VALUE AND BELIEF SYSTEMS
OF BEHAVIORAL SCIENTIST CHANGE AGENTS

While scientific inquiry, ideally, is value free, the applications of science are not value free.[8] Applied behavioral scientist–organization development consultants tend to subscribe to a comparable set of values, although we should avoid the trap of assuming that they constitute a completely homogeneous group. From our experience, they do not.

One value, to which many behavioral scientist–change agents tend to give high priority, is that the needs and aspirations of human beings are the reasons for organized effort in society. They tend, therefore, to be developmental in their outlook and concerned with the long-range opportunities for the personal growth of people in organizations.

This humanistic orientation creates a self-fulfilling prophecy. The belief that people are important tends to result in their being important. The belief that people can grow and develop in terms of personal and organizational competency tends to produce this result. Thus, values and beliefs can be self-fulfilling, and the question becomes, "What do you choose to want to believe?" While this position can be naïve in the sense of not seeing the real world, nevertheless, behavioral scientist–change agents—these authors at least—tend to place a value on optimism. It is a kind of optimism that says people can do a better job of goal setting and facing up to and solving problems, not an optimism that says the number of problems is diminishing.

A second value that tends to be held by change agents is that work and life can become richer and more meaningful, and organized effort more effective and enjoyable, if feelings and sentiments are permitted to be a more legitimate part of the culture of organizations. This value, of course, like any other, can be held in excess with a lack of attention to organizational realities. For example, the OD consultant may be overly zealous in promoting openness in a conflict situation. A reality may be that the internal reward system rewards winners of internal struggles regardless of the human resources wasted in the process.

A third value held by change agents is a commitment to an action

[8] Parts of this section are drawn from Wendell French, *The Personnel Management Process,* 2nd ed. (Boston: Houghton Mifflin Company, 1970), Chap. 28; and Wendell French, "Organization Development Objectives, Assumptions and Strategies," *California Management Review,* 12 (Winter 1969), 23–34.

role, along with a commitment to research, in an effort to improve the effectiveness of organizations.[9] Although many change agents are perhaps overly action oriented in terms of the utilization of their time, as a group they are paying more and more attention to research and to the examination of ideas.[10]

This importance placed on research and inquiry raises the question whether the assumptions stated in this chapter are values, theory, or "facts." In our judgment, a substantial body of experience and knowledge, including research on leadership, suggests that there is considerable evidence for these assumptions. To conclude that these assumptions were facts, laws, or principles, however, would be to contradict the value placed by behavioral scientists on continuous research and inquiry. Thus, the assumptions we have stated should be considered theoretical statements based on provisional data.

Finally, a value frequently attributed to applied behavioral scientists is a presumed value placed on democratization of organizations or on "power equalization." While most probably would place value on a democratic-participative way of life, most would not, for example, subscribe to the wisdom of all organizational members electing the president of a corporation. They would, however, subscribe to this procedure as it related to the central government of the broader society.

This is where we are on the issue. As organization development consultants, we do not see our role as power equalizers. We do, however, believe that most organizations can profitably learn to be more responsive to organizational members and that all parties concerned can learn to be more skillful in this responsiveness. A major route to increased organizational effectiveness is through creating conditions under which organization members can make larger contributions to organizational goals. But this may mean that managers will need to augment the authority of their positions with additional skills in being more responsive to the human-social subsystem.

Parenthetically, it should be added that it is important for each behavioral scientist–change agent to make his values and beliefs visible to both himself and his client. Neither party can learn to trust the other

---

[9] Bennis sees three major approaches to planned organizational change, with the behavioral scientists associated with each having "a deep concern with applying social science knowledge to create more viable social systems; a commitment to action, as well as to research ... and a belief that improved interpersonal and group relationships will ultimately lead to better organizational performance." Warren G. Bennis, "A New Role for the Behavioral Sciences: Effecting Organizational Change," *Administrative Science Quarterly,* 8 (September 1963), 157–58.

[10] For a discussion of some of the problems and dilemmas in behavioral science research, see Chris Argyris, "Creating Effective Relationships in Organizations," in Richard N. Adams and Jack J. Preiss, eds., *Human Organization Research* (Homewood, Ill.: The Dorsey Press, 1960), pp. 109–23.

adequately without such exposure—hidden agendas handicap both trust building and mutual learning. Perhaps more pragmatically, organization development change efforts tend to fail if strategies or techniques are applied unilaterally and without open collaboration.

SUMMARY

Organization development activities rest on a number of assumptions about people as individuals, in groups, and in total systems, about the transactional nature of organization improvement, and about values. These assumptions tend to be humanistic, developmental, and optimistic. Assumptions and values held by change agents need to be made explicit, both for enhancing working relationships with clients and for continuous testing through practice and research.

Some assumptions stem from a "systems" view of organizations. In the next chapter, we will elaborate upon some of these systems concepts.

7

Relevant Systems Concepts

We have already used the word *system* and would like to elaborate on the concept because it has considerable utility in helping pose questions about organization development and in planning change strategies. Although a systems view of organizations and change will be drawn upon throughout this book, we try to be explicit about its relevance in this chapter. We first look at some definitions and descriptions and then move on to a further discussion of the relevance of these ideas to organization development.

THE CONCEPT OF SYSTEM

Fagen defines *system* as "a set of objects together with relationships between the objects and between their attributes." [1] Bertalanffy refers to a system as a set of "elements standing in interaction." [2] Johnson, Kast, and Rosenzweig define system as "an organized or complex whole; an assemblage or combination of things or parts forming a complex or unitary whole." [3] Thus, *system* denotes interdependency or interaction of components or parts, and an identifiable wholeness or Gestalt. Organizations are systems, and the aspects of interdependency and interaction of com-

[1] See A. D. Hall and R. E. Fagen, "Definition of a System," *General Systems.* Yearbook of the Society for the Advancement of General Systems Theory, 1 (1956), 18–28.

[2] *Ibid.,* pp. 1–10.

[3] See R. A. Johnson, F. E. Kast, and J. E. Rosenzweig, *The Theory and Management of Systems* (New York: McGraw-Hill Book Company, 1963), pp. 4–6. 91, 92.

74

ponents and of wholeness are very important dimensions in organization development, as we will see later.

ADDITIONAL CHARACTERISTICS OF SYSTEMS

Other dimensions of systems are also relevant. Systems in operation (active systems), such as organizations, can be viewed as a linkage of *input* flows (energy, materials, or information) from *sources* in the external environment, a transforming mechanism (a machine or a technical-human organization), and flows of *outputs* or *outcomes,* provided to *users.* The system may include one or more *feedback* mechanisms for self-regulation. For example, signals from the internal or external environment that the output is substandard could result in changes in either the transforming mechanism or the inputs, or both. (See Figure 7-1.)

Each of these components needs to be effectively managed and linked if there is to be a healthy organization. For example, to focus most attention on the technical-human organization (transforming mechanism) and to ignore how customers or clientele are reacting to the product (the user-output relationship) can lead to serious consequences. To illustrate,

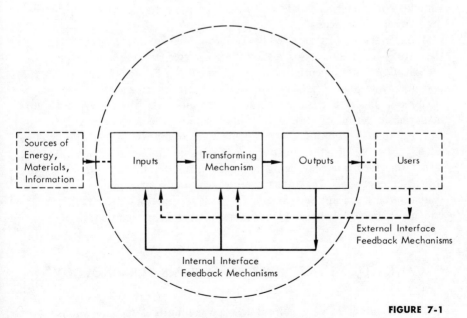

FIGURE 7-1

DIAGRAM OF A SYSTEM IN INTERACTION
WITH ITS ENVIRONMENT

lack of attention by the American automobile industry to public interest in economy cars led to lost opportunity for several years. We recall a top executive of a major automobile corporation saying some years ago that Volkswagen owners "were crazy"; a few years later his company was spending millions of dollars competing with Volkswagen and other non–United States manufacturers of economy cars.

Similarly, to focus on seeking sources of funding (input) or to concentrate on marketing (output) to the extent of ignoring the effectiveness of the technical-human organization can also have disastrous results. As an illustration, we have seen a chief executive of an organization almost destroy it by spending almost all his energy on external matters while paying inadequate attention to the quality of internal communications and administration. As a consequence, all his key subordinates were frustrated, were often in serious conflict with each other, and harbored a growing disillusionment with his leadership. Both illustrations are examples of inadequate attention to feedback mechanisms and to managing the interrelationships of system components. Or, in organizational jargon, these are illustrations of inadequate management of the *interface* between subparts of a system or between a system and its external environment. (The second illustration, in particular, is an instance in which OD technology might have helped avoid an organizational crisis; OD techniques also have been used successfully in managing external interfaces.)

To elaborate further, while systems differ in the degree to which they are in an open versus a closed state, organizations and subparts of organizations are essentially *open systems* in that they exist in interdependent, exchange relationships with their environments. The more effectively these exchange relationships—that is, the interfaces—are managed in terms of utilizing inputs, the less the system is subject to *entropy,* that is, running down, becoming marginal or obsolete, or going out of existence. In the illustration of the automobile company, the external interface was not being managed properly. In the illustration of the chief executive, the internal interfaces between organizational subsystems—between himself and the board of directors, between himself and his staff, and between departments—were being ignored.

ORGANIZATIONS DESCRIBED IN SYSTEMS TERMINOLOGY

Although it is very helpful to view subunits of organizations—for example, departments and divisions—as subsystems, we also find it useful to think of organizations as consisting of a number of significant interacting variables which cut across or are common to all subunits. These variables have to do with goals, tasks, technology, human-social organization, structure, and external interface relationships. Thus, we can visualize organizations as consisting of a goal subsystem, a task subsystem, a technological subsystem, a human-social subsystem, a structural subsystem, and an external interface subsystem.[4] (See Figure 7-2.) All can be influenced by OD efforts, although some are more likely to be the initial change target, as we will see later.

This way of viewing the organization is more elaborate than the ideas implicit in Figure 7-1, but it includes them all. For example, the concept of feedback is included in Figure 7-2 in the notion of the external interface system, and in the notion of the internal communications subsystem. (What is a "system" or a "subsystem" is purely relative and depends upon at what level of abstraction or level of complexity one is focusing his analysis.)

To elaborate on this way of viewing organizations, the *goal subsystem* consists of one or more (usually several) interrelated superordinate objectives or goals, usually set forth in the organization's charter or mission statement, plus the subgoals of units and programs stemming from or forming the superordinate goals. Although corporate goals are frequently reported in terms of profit objectives, even a superficial probing finds most business executives talking about the production of particular kinds of goods or services at a profit. Most are very conscious of the importance of satisfying certain customer or client needs if they are to satisfy their own. Furthermore, significant aspects of the goal system are the subunit or program goals which either stem from or act interdependently with overall goals.[5] The interrelationship between these levels of goals typically is an area of considerable tension in organizations and requires extensive managing.

The *technological subsystem* consists of tools, machines, procedures, methods, and technical knowledge. In essence, this subsystem consists

[4] This view of an organization is an elaboration of the models described by Leavitt and Seiler. The former views industrial organizations as complex systems with four major "interacting variables": task, structural, technological, and human; the latter views organizations as sociotechnical systems comprised of four major variables: human, technological, organizational, and social. See Harold J. Leavitt, "Applied Organizational Change in Industry; Structural, Technological and Humanistic Approaches," in James G. March, *Handbook of Organizations* (Rand McNally & Co., 1965), pp. 1144–45; and John A. Seiler, *Systems Analysis in Organizational Behavior* (Homewood, Ill.: Richard D. Irwin, Inc., 1967), pp. 23–29. See also E. L. Trist *et al., Organizational Choice* (London: Tavistock Publications, 1963). Katz and Kahn refer to technical, maintenance, supportive, institutional, adaptive, and managerial subsystems. Daniel Katz and Robert L. Kahn, *The Social Psychology of Organization* (New York: John Wiley & Sons, Inc., 1966), p. 456.

[5] To be more specific, we can also think about goals in terms of a descending level of abstractions, e.g., end-result, strategic, tactical, and program goals.

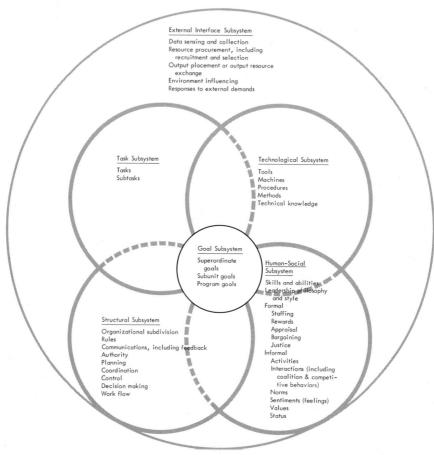

External Interface Subsystem

Data sensing and collection
Resource procurement, including
 recruitment and selection
Output placement or output resource
 exchange
Environment influencing
Responses to external demands

Task Subsystem

Tasks
Subtasks

Technological Subsystem

Tools
Machines
Procedures
Methods
Technical knowledge

Goal Subsystem

Superordinate
 goals
Subunit goals
Program goals

Human–Social Subsystem

Skills and abilities
Leadership philosophy
 and style
Formal
 Staffing
 Rewards
 Appraisal
 Bargaining
 Justice
Informal
 Activities
 Interactions (including
  coalition & competi-
  tive behaviors)
 Norms
 Sentiments (feelings)
 Values
 Status

Structural Subsystem

Organizational subdivision
Rules
Communications, including feedback
Authority
Planning
Coordination
Control
Decision making
Work flow

FIGURE 7-2

Major Organizational Subsystems

of the artifacts and knowledge that have been assembled to produce an end product, and it stems largely from the goal subsystem.

The *task subsystem* consists of the subdivision of the total work to be performed into those tasks and subtasks that need to be accomplished by organization members to produce the end product. The actual tasks to be done are highly dependent upon the technological subsystem. For example, the kinds of machines or tools used will extensively influence the tasks to be performed.

The *structural subsystem* is highly influenced by the technological subsystem and consists of task groupings such as units, departments, or divisions. Interrelated with such task groupings is the design of the work flow, that is, where a partially completed product goes next, and so forth. Also included in the structural subsystem are work rules, such as beginning and ending hours; the authority system, for example, who reports to whom, and who can exercise sanctions toward whom; and procedures and practices relative to communicating, planning, coordination, control, and decision making. These three subsystems—technological, task, and structural—are obviously highly interdependent.

The *human-social subsystem* can be viewed as consisting of four aspects: the *skills and abilities* of organizational members, the *leadership philosophy and style,* a *formal* subsystem, and an *informal* subsystem. Skills and abilities are included because the capabilities of organization members pervade all organizational subsystems. While leadership philosophy and style can be considered one aspect of skills and abilities, we choose to separate out these dimensions because they are so highly interrelated with such matters as the way decisions are made and the degree of concern for human values expressed in the organization. By formal subsystem is meant personnel subsystems, such as staffing (assignment, transfer, promotion, separation), rewards (financial and otherwise), and appraisal (performance review and the communication of that review); bargaining subsystems (formalized collective bargaining or quasi-bargaining relationships); and the system of organizational justice (mechanisms for equitable treatment and for remedying wrongs, for example, appeal systems). The informal subsystem consists of nonprogrammed activities and interactions, including resistant behaviors and coalition and competitive behaviors; group norms; sentiments (feelings); values; and status. (See Chapter 2.)

The *external interface subsystem* consists of data sensing and gathering (e.g., market or public reaction surveys); resource procurement (e.g., recruitment and selection, and purchasing); output placement or exchanges of outputs for resources; environment influencing (e.g., advertising, public relations, pollution control); and responses to external demands. The latter has recently become a very conspicuous and impactive aspect of organizational life. The incidents are too numerous to recount: governmental pressures on hiring practices, sit-ins in university presidents' offices, policemen on strike, marches to city halls, picketing of business firms and of conventions, partial consumer boycotts, and the like. How all these kinds of interface problems are managed can have important consequences for the success, health, or viability of an organization.

RELEVANCE TO ORGANIZATION DEVELOPMENT: ADDITIONAL COMMENTS

The above discussion of systems concepts and a systems view of organizations leads to several generalizations about organization development. First, *because organizational subsystems exist in a highly interdependent state, system-wide changes may occur by introducing changes in any one of these subsystems.* Thus, OD interventions need to be based on a diagnosis of the consequences throughout the system of different options open to the change agent and key clients.[6]

Second, *the initial vehicle for organization development efforts—for improvements in any or all of the organizational subsystems—tends to be an intervention in the human-social and the structural subsystems.* That is, the sentiments and attitudes of organizational members are tapped relative to problems they see in the organization, and in this process the communications and perhaps even the authority and control subsystems are altered. A prior condition may be some change in leadership philosophy or style.

As a third generalization, *there is an immediate interrelated impact between the human-social and the structural subsystems.* For example, the moment group members start trying to understand the norms under which they have been operating, their communications and probably their decision making will be affected. When a manager begins to listen to and understand feelings, the authority structure begins to shift. Reciprocally, the outcome of a manager altering his communications style to a more inquiring and understanding-seeking stance is likely to be a positive shift in subordinate feelings.

And fourth, *while the initial vehicle for organization development efforts tends to be an intervention in the human-social and the structural subsystems, there is likely to be either a direct or an indirect confrontation of the goal, task, technological, and external interface systems, plus the human-social and the structural subsystems themselves.* To elaborate, unit or organizational goals are frequently reviewed and modified in "team-building" sessions. Using the Chapter 1 examples, some attention was given to organizational goals in Illustration 1 ("Problems in a Business Firm"), in Illustration 2 ("Start-up of a New Junior High School"), and in Illustration 3 ("Departure from Tradition in a Division of a Large Corporation").

---

[6] O'Connell appropriately challenges the idea that there is "one best way" of changing organizations and emphasizes that the consultant should choose his role and intervention strategy on the basis of "the conditions existing when he enters the client system." Jeremiah J. O'Connell, *Managing Organizational Innovation* (Homewood, Ill.: Richard D. Irwin, Inc., 1968), pp. 10–11.

Further, the external interface subsystem is frequently examined in OD efforts. In Illustration 1 there was a review of customer relationships. In some OD efforts, key people involved in the interface are brought together to work on mutual problems with the help of a third party. For example, manufacturers and salespeople from one organization may be brought together to meet with key people from a customer organization.

Although extensive technological changes are typically not made directly through OD interventions, team member reactions to obstacles in carrying out tasks may result in changes in procedures or equipment (technological subsystem). For example, in the instance of Illustration 1 in Chapter 1, action plans that emerged from the workshop included changing procedures having to do with customer complaints. In Illustration 3 ("Departure from Tradition in a Division of a Large Corporation"), action steps included adding direct telephone lines between plants to avoid switchboard delays.

Indirectly, the task subsystem is always modified in OD efforts. For example, in Illustration 5 ("A New Plant Manager"), the very fact that subordinate managers were involved in group sessions served to alter the mix of tasks and the nature of their jobs. Very simply, the planning and decision-making components were being enlarged. More directly, the task subsystem is frequently altered through an exploration of group members' expectations of each other. This occurred in Illustrations 2 and 3, and in Illustration 4 ("Organizational Improvement in an Indian Tribe").

Thus, organization development efforts may be somewhat more of a total or Gestalt kind of consulting than has sometimes been recognized. It does not suffice, for example, to say that OD focuses on "human relations" or "interpersonal relations" unless, of course, the consultant's style or the client's needs keep the change efforts in these realms.

Indicative of this Gestalt approach is a fairly common question asked by change agents in the data-gathering phase of an organization development intervention: "What do you see as getting in the way of getting the job done the way you would like to see it get done?" The responses can pertain to any one of the organizational subsystems as described in Figure 7-2. We should, however, recognize the "set" that respondents will have; if there has been appropriate pre-work, a change agent will be perceived as an organizational facilitator, not as a technological expert.[7]

---

[7] To elaborate, the change agent may assist a unit in facing up to and making decisions about technology, but he will tend to stay out of making technological or other prescriptions. He may, however, suggest additional options for consideration if the problem area is within his area of expertise. A major trap for the OD consultant is to permit his client to place him in the role of the expert who is supposed to solve problems *for* the organization. The OD consultant is likely to lose his effectiveness quickly if he gets into this bind. See Chapter 16 for a further discussion of this point.

Finally, to elaborate on another concept, "openness," feedback and understanding are directly related to the degree of system openness. While organizations are relatively open systems in contrast to, for example, a hydraulic system, they do differ markedly in the degree to which relevant (or potentially relevant) data are shared between people and between subparts of the system. A central issue in organizational life, then, is the degree to which members of the organization are permitted to communicate fully with each other about the various organizational subsystems and the degree to which such communications are facilitated. *This issue is at the heart of organization development; the decision to explore the usefulness of an OD strategy is to decide to examine the utility or the wisdom of enlarging the data base used by organization members in decision making. And since fuller information and more complete understanding lead to more mutual influence, the issue becomes one of whether or not the key power figures wish to enlarge the domain of mutual influence within the organization.*

Parenthetically, at another level is the issue of the *quality* of system openness and the quality of the feedback mechanisms. In particular, to what degree is the OD effort to become truly collaborative? The more secret or unilateral the efforts, the more manipulative; the more open and truly participative, the more the efforts are nonmanipulative and the more viable the intervention is likely to be. But openness can be either constructive or destructive. Are the feedback mechanisms developmental or are they punitive and reductive? Thus, both the extent and the quality of system openness are important issues in OD, as will be implicit throughout this book.

SUMMARY

The concept of system, which is a major assumption in organization development efforts, denotes interdependency of components and an identifiable wholeness or Gestalt.

Organizations can be viewed as consisting of goal, task, technological, human-social, structural, and external interface subsystems existing in a state of dynamic interdependence. Such concepts as interface, entropy, feedback, and openness are useful in understanding organizations and in raising issues relative to improvement strategies. For example, issues pertaining to both the extent and the quality of organizational feedback mechanisms are important.

The initial vehicles for organization development efforts tend to be the human-social and the structural subsystems, that is, the communications and feedback systems and the attitude and sentiment components of the informal system. However, these become vehicles for confronting problems in any of the major organizational subsystems. The OD process sets off interdependent changes in the human-social and the structural subsystems, and quite likely in all the major organizational subsystems. The OD consultant concentrates on facilitating problem solving relative to these subsystems and avoids being placed in the role of adviser-expert.

8

Action Research
and Organization Development

A basic model underlying most organization development activities is the action research model—a data-based, problem-solving model that replicates the steps involved in the scientific method of inquiry. Three processes are involved in action research: data collection, feedback of the data to the clients, and action planning based on the data.[1] Action research is both an *approach* to problem solving—a model or a paradigm, and a problem-solving *process*—a series of activities and events.

We examine the action research model in this chapter for two main reasons: first, the importance of action research as an underpinning for OD seems not to be appreciated sufficiently; and second, there seems to be some misunderstanding about what action research really is. We address these two issues in this chapter. Action research from the points of view of a process and an approach are given, followed by remarks on the history and the kinds of action research. The role and appropriate use of action research in organization development conclude the chapter.

ACTION RESEARCH AS A PROCESS

Action research may be described as a process, that is, as an ongoing series of events and actions. Used in this way, we define *action research* as follows: action research is the process of systematically collecting research data about an ongoing system relative to some objective, goal, or need of that system; feeding these data back into the system; taking actions by altering selected variables within the system based both on the

[1] Richard Beckhard, *Organization Development: Strategies and Models* (Reading, Mass.: Addison-Wesley Publishing Company, 1969), p. 28.

data and on hypotheses; and evaluating the results of actions by collecting more data. This definition characterizes action research in terms of the activities comprising the process: first a static picture is taken of an organization; on the basis of "what exists," hunches and hypotheses suggest actions; these actions typically entail manipulating some variable in the system that is under the control of the action researcher (this often means doing something differently from the way it has always been done); later, a second static picture is taken of the system to examine the effects of the actions taken. These steps are the same steps we have described as being what the OD practitioner does as he attempts to improve an organization's functioning.

Several authors have noted the importance of viewing action research as a process. Stephen Corey, an early advocate of action research in education, states: "The process by which practitioners attempt to study their problems scientifically in order to guide, correct, and evaluate their decisions and actions is what a number of people have called action research." [2] Elsewhere Corey defines the term more in terms of a practitioners' tool: "Action research in education is research undertaken by practitioners in order that they may improve their practices." [3] In a study of the Tremont Hotel in Chicago, William F. Whyte and Edith L. Hamilton described their work as follows:

> What was the project? It was an action-research program for management. We developed a process for applying human relations research findings to the changing of organization behavior. The word *process* is important, for this was not a one-shot affair. The project involved a continuous gathering and analysis of human relations research data and the feeding of the findings into the organization in such a way as to change behavior.[4]

This study by Whyte and Hamilton is a particularly cogent example of the role of action research in improving an organization. Although the study itself was conducted in 1945 and 1946—before the term *organization development* was introduced—it would be considered an OD program today, even though it was based solely on an action research model.

In Figure 8-1 French presents a diagram of the process of action research as it relates to organization development.[5] His diagram points up

[2] Stephen M. Corey, *Action Research to Improve School Practices* (New York: Bureau of Publications, Teachers College, Columbia University, 1953), p. 6.

[3] *Ibid.*, p. 141.

[4] William F. Whyte and Edith L. Hamilton, *Action Research for Management* (Homewood, Ill.: Irwin-Dorsey Press, 1964), pp. 1–2.

[5] Wendell French, "Organization Development Objectives, Assumptions, and Strategies," *California Management Review*, 12 (Winter 1969), 23–34. Figure used with permission.

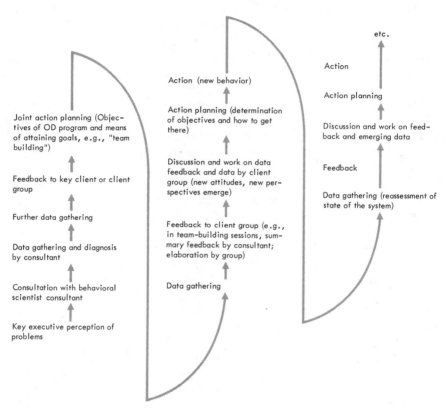

FIGURE 8-1

AN ACTION RESEARCH MODEL FOR ORGANIZATION DEVELOPMENT

the iterative or cyclical nature of the process. He clarifies the model as follows:

> The key aspects of the model are *diagnosis, data gathering, feedback to the client group, data discussion and work by the client group, action planning, and action*. The sequence tends to be cyclical, with the focus on new or advanced problems as the client group learns to work more effectively together.[6]

Action research is a process in two different ways: it is a sequence of events and activities *within* each iteration (data collection, feedback and working the data, and action based on the data); and it is a *cycle* of iterations of these activities sometimes treating the same problem through several cycles and sometimes moving to different problems in each cycle. Both aspects point up the ongoing nature of action research.

[6] *Ibid.*, p. 26.

ACTION RESEARCH AS AN APPROACH

Action research may also be described as an approach to problem solving, thus suggesting its usefulness as a model, a guide, or a paradigm. Used in this way, *action research* may be defined as follows: action research is the application of the scientific method of fact-finding and experimentation to practical problems requiring action solutions and involving the collaboration and cooperation of scientists, practitioners, and laymen. Viewing action research from this perspective points up some additional features that are important.

Action research was the conceptual model for an early organization improvement program in a series of oil refineries. Herbert Shepard, one of the behavioral scientists involved in that program, defines the nature of action research as follows:

> The action research model is a normative model for learning, or a model for planned change. Its main features are these. In front of intelligent human action there should be an objective, be it ever so fuzzy or distorted. And in advance of human action there should be planning, although knowledge of paths to the objective is always inadequate. Action itself should be taken a step at a time, and after each step it is well to do some fact-finding. The fact-finding may disclose whether the objective is realistic, whether it is nearer or more distant than before, whether it needs alteration. Through fact-finding, the present situation can be assessed, and this information, together with information about the objective, can be used in planning the second step. Movement toward an objective consists of a series of such cycles of planning—acting—fact-finding—planning.[7]

Shepard diagrams his concept of the action research model as shown in Figure 8-2.[8]

Shepard highlights the relations between goals (objectives), planning, and action in his diagram—a point we think is a very important feature of action research. And both he and French emphasize that action research is research inextricably linked to action; furthermore, it is research-with-a-purpose, that is to say, to guide present and future action.

In an action research approach, the role of the consultant/change agent takes on a special form, as shown by Shepard:

[7] Herbert A. Shepard, "An Action Research Model," in *An Action Research Program for Organization Improvement* (Ann Arbor: The Foundation for Research on Human Behavior, University of Michigan, 1960), pp. 33–34.

[8] Figure 8-2 is from Herbert A. Shepard, "An Action Research Model," in *An Action Research Program for Organization Improvement* (Ann Arbor: The Foundation for Research on Human Behavior, 1960), p. 33, and is used with permission.

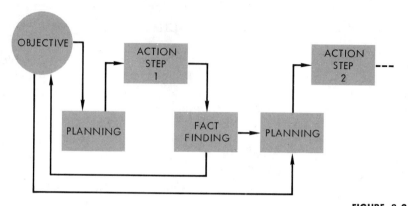

FIGURE 8-2

ACTION RESEARCH MODEL

The role is to help the manager plan his actions and design his fact-finding procedures in such a way that he can learn from them, to serve such ends as becoming a more skillfull manager, setting more realistic objectives, discovering better ways of organizing. In this sense, the staff concerned with follow-up are research consultants. Their task is to help managers formulate management problems as experiments.[9]

By viewing action research as an approach to problem solving we have noted the following features: the normative nature of this model, the importance and centrality of goals and objectives, and the different role requirements of the consultant/change agent vis-à-vis the clients. Two additional features deserve discussion—first, the elements of the action research model that link it to the scientific method of inquiry; and second, the collaborative relation between scientists, practitioners, and laymen that often is a component of action research.

The paradigm for problematical inquiry that serves both as the model for the scientific method and as the model for action research was introduced by the philosopher John Dewey in his book *How We Think*.[10] He identified the following five phases of reflective thinking: suggestion, intellectualization, hypothesizing, reasoning, and testing the hypothesis by action. This approach to problem solving is translated into the scientific method steps as follows. First the scientist is confronted with a *problem, obstacle, or new idea* that he wants to understand (Dewey's suggestion phase). He identifies the problem, intellectualizes about it (what we

[9] *Ibid.*, p. 34.

[10] John Dewey, *How We Think*, rev. ed. (New York: D. C. Heath & Company, 1933).

usually call "thinking"), and arrives at the point where he can formulate a *hypothesis* about the problem. (A *hypothesis* is a conjectural statement positing the relations between two or more phenomena, usually referred to as a "cause" and an "effect.") The next step, a critical one, consists of the scientist *reasoning or deducing the consequences of the hypothesis.* The final step consists of *observing, testing, or experimenting* to see if the relation between the two phenomena expressed in the hypothesis is verified or disconfirmed.[11]

These steps for the scientific method are identical with the steps outlined by Corey for action research in which he says:

The significant elements of a design for action research are:

1. The identification of a problem area about which an individual or a group is sufficiently concerned to want to take some action.
2. The selection of a specific problem and the formulation of a hypothesis or prediction that implies a goal and a procedure for reaching it. This specific goal must be viewed in relation to the total situation.
3. The careful recording of actions taken and the accumulation of evidence to determine the degree to which the goal has been achieved.
4. The inference from this evidence of generalizations regarding the relation between the actions and the desired goal.
5. The continuous retesting of these generalizations in action situations.

If the problem under attack is one of concern to many people, or if it is likely that the experiment will affect many people, the action research should involve these people. It then becomes *cooperative* action research.[12]

An example applying action research to a typical organizational problem might be helpful. Suppose that the problem is unproductive weekly staff meetings—they are poorly attended; members express low commitment and involvement in them; a low level of activity and interaction is common in them; and they are generally agreed to be unproductive. Suppose also that you are the manager in charge of both the meetings and the staff and that you desire to make the meetings a vital, productive instrument for your organization. Following the action research model, the first step is to gather data about the *status quo*. Assume this has been done, and the data suggest the meetings are generally disliked and regarded as unproductive. The next step is to search for causes of the problem and to

[11] Based on a discussion in Fred N. Kerlinger, *Foundations of Behavioral Research* (New York: Holt, Rinehart & Winston, Inc., 1964), pp. 13–17.
[12] Corey, *Action Research to Improve School Practices*, pp. 40–41.

generate one or more hypotheses from which you deduce the consequences that will allow the hypotheses to be tested. Say you come up with four hypotheses as listed below. Note the very important feature that an action research hypothesis consists of two aspects: a goal and an action or procedure for achieving that goal.

1. Staff meetings will be more productive if I solicit and use agenda topics from the staff rather than have the agenda made up just by me.
2. Staff meetings will be more productive if I rotate the chairmanship of the meeting among the staff rather than my always being chairman.
3. Staff meetings will be more productive if we have them twice a week instead of only once a week.
4. I have always run the staff meetings in a brisk "all-business–no-nonsense" fashion; perhaps if I (*a*) loosen up on what can be discussed and how, (*b*) encourage more discussion, (*c*) listen to what is said more carefully, and (*d*) am more open about how I am reacting to what is being said, then staff meetings will be more productive.

Each of these action research hypotheses has a goal, or objective (better staff meeting productivity), and each has an action, or procedure, for achieving the goal. Additional work would be done to clarify and specify the goal and the actions in more detail, and then the hypotheses would be systematically tested (implemented) and evaluated for their effects through data collection.

Another distinguishing feature of action research is collaboration between individuals inside the system—clients—and individuals outside the system—change agents or researchers. Havelock, for example, defines action research as

> the collaboration of researcher and practitioner in the diagnosis and evaluation of problems existing in the practice setting. . . . It provides the cooperating practitioner system with scientific data about its own operation which may be used for self-evaluation.[13]

Elsewhere Havelock discusses "collaborative Action Inquiry," which

> is similar to "action research." However, this model places greater emphasis on service to the practitioner system and on the collaborative teaming of research and practitioner. The inquiry team collaborates on defining goals, on all phases of the research, and on change strategies. . . .[14]

[13] Ronald G. Havelock, *Planning for Innovation through Dissemination and Utilization of Knowledge* (Ann Arbor: Institute for Social Research, The University of Michigan, 1969), pp. 9–33.
[14] *Ibid.*

Almost all authors stress the collaborative nature of action research, with some seeing it as the primary reason for the model's efficacy.[15]

It is a widely held belief that people tend to support what they have helped to create. Such a belief is highly congruent with the collaborative aspect of the action research model and impels practitioners and researchers alike to cooperate extensively with client system members. Such a point of view implies that the client system members and the researcher should jointly define the problems they want to address, should define the methods used for data collection, should identify the hypotheses relevant to the situations, and should evaluate the consequences of actions taken. We believe this collaborative ingredient of action research is particularly important in organization development and give additional attention to it in the next section.

THE HISTORY, USE, AND VARIETIES OF ACTION RESEARCH

John Dewey translated the scientific method of problem solving into terms understandable by practitioners and laymen, and these seminal ideas were incorporated into action research several years later. The origin of action research can be traced to two independent sources. One source, John Collier, was a man of practical affairs; the other, Kurt Lewin, was a man of science. John Collier was commissioner of Indian Affairs from 1933 to 1945, a role in which he had to diagnose problems and recommend remedial programs for the improvement of race relations. Collier found that effecting changes in ethnic relations was an extremely difficult process and required *joint effort* on the part of the scientist (researcher), the administrator (practitioner), and the layman (client).

> Principle seven I would call the first and the last: that research and then more research is essential to the program, that in the ethnic field research can be made a tool of action essential to all the other tools, indeed, that it ought to be the master tool. But we had in mind a particular kind of research, or, if you will, particular conditions. We had in mind research impelled from central areas of needed action. And since action is by nature not only specialized but also integrative to more than the specialities, our needed research must be of the integrative sort. Again, since the findings of the research must be carried into effect by the administrator and the layman, and must be criticized by them through their experience, the administrator and the layman must them-

---

[15] In this regard, the work of Collier (cited later in this chapter), Corey, and Lippitt (cited later) indicates a heavy emphasis on the importance of collaboration between all the individuals affected by a change project of this nature.

selves participate creatively in the research, impelled as it is from their own area of need.[16]

Collier called this form of research *action research*. Taking effective actions requires research directed to important practical problems, and the solutions must be relevant and feasible. To be able to implement a good action plan also requires cooperation of the client. Action research seemed to afford a means to mesh these diverse elements.

The other major source for theory and practice of action research, Kurt Lewin, was a social psychologist who was profoundly interested in applying social science knowledge to help solve social problems. In the mid-forties and early fifties, Lewin and his students conducted action research projects in many different behavioral domains: Lewin applied action research principles to intergroup relations and to changing eating habits; Lippitt, and Lippitt and Radke, applied the tool to an extensive community relations project; Bavelas conducted an action research project on leadership training; Coch and French applied the model to studying resistance to change in an industrial plant.[17]

Lewin's work with social agency practitioners engaged in eradicating prejudice led him to conclude that research to help the practitioner was imperative. His answer to the need was action research. Only by conducting research could action people generate standards by which to measure progress. Speaking to this problem he said:

> In a field that lacks objective standards of achievement, no learning can take place. If we cannot judge whether an action has led forward or backward, if we have no criteria for evaluating the relation between effort and achievement, there is nothing to prevent us from making the wrong conclusions and to encourage the wrong work habits. Realistic fact-finding and evaluation is a prerequisite for any learning. Social research should be one of the top priorities for the practical job of improving intergroup relations.[18]

For the Lewin group, action research represented a linking of experimentation and application, and at the same time, men of science and men of action. As an example Lippitt, in the preface to his book on community

[16] John Collier, "United States Indian Administration as a Laboratory of Ethnic Relations," *Social Research,* 12 (May 1945), 275–76.

[17] The relevant sources for Lewin's work are as follows: Kurt Lewin, "Action Research and Minority Problems," *Journal of Social Issues,* 2, No. 4 (1946), 34–46; *Resolving Social Conflicts* (New York: Harper & Bros., 1948); in addition, Ronald Lippitt, *Training in Community Relations* (New York: Harper & Row, Publishers, 1951); Ronald Lippitt and Marion Radke, "New Trends in the Investigation of Prejudice," *Annals of the American Academy of Political and Social Science,* 244 (March 1946), 167–76; Lester Coch and J. R. P. French, Jr., "Overcoming Resistance to Change," *Human Relations,* 1 (1948, 512–32.

[18] Lewin, "Action Research and Minority Problems," p. 35.

action research, states: "Bringing together in a single cooperative adventure the skills and resources of both men of science, and men of action, this project is an example of 'action research.' " [19]

Other noteworthy action research projects may be found in the literature.[20] Whyte and Hamilton studied the effects of human relations practices in a large hotel; Elliott Jaques used the action research model in effecting change in the culture of a factory in England; Cyril Sofer applied the methods in three diverse organizations undergoing change for which he was a researcher-consultant; Floyd Mann, and Seashore and Bowers, applied the methods to industrial plants undergoing changes in leadership; Shepard, Katzell, and others, working at a large refinery, used action research to effect a planned change program; Morse and Reimer's field experiment investigating leadership styles and participation in an insurance company is an example of action research; and Miles, Hornstein, Callahan, Calder, and Schiavo used action research to investigate the processes of self-renewal in a school system. The payoff from a good action research project is high: practical problems get solved, a contribution is made to theory and to practice in behavioral science, and greater understanding grows between scientist, practitioner, and layman. Some varieties of action research emphasize one kind of payoff over others, as we see in the next section.

Action research projects may be directed toward diverse goals, thereby giving rise to several variations of the model. Lewin, for example, suggested two broad categories of action research: the investigation of general laws and the diagnosis of a specific situation.[21] The study of general laws leads to contributions to theory and practice, and to generalizations about natural phenomena; the diagnosis of a specific situation leads to solving immediate, practical problems.

[19] Lippitt, *Training in Community Relations,* p. ix.

[20] Whyte and Hamilton, *Action Research for Management;* Elliott Jaques, *The Changing Culture of a Factory* (New York: Dryden Press, 1952); Cyril Sofer, *The Organization from Within* (Chicago: Quadrangle Books, 1962); Floyd Mann, "Studying and Creating Change: A Means to Understanding Social Organization," in C. M. Arensberg *et al.*, eds., *Research in Industrial Human Relations* (New York: Harper & Row, Publishers, 1957); and S. E. Seashore and D. G. Bowers, *Changing the Structure and Functioning of an Organization,* Monograph No. 33 (Ann Arbor: Survey Research Center, The University of Michigan, 1963). Herbert A. Shepard and Raymond A. Katzell are two of the writers for the book *An Action Research Program for Organization Improvement, op. cit.* Nancy Morse and E. Reimer, "The Experimental Change of a Major Organizational Variable," *Journal of Abnormal and Social Psychology,* 52 (January 1956), 120–29. Matthew Miles, Harvey Hornstein, Daniel Callahan, Paula Calder, and R. Steven Schiavo, "The Consequence of Survey Feedback: Theory and Evaluation," in Warren Bennis, Kenneth Benne, and Robert Chin, *The Planning of Change,* 2nd ed. (New York: Holt, Rinehart & Winston, Inc., 1969), pp. 457–68.

[21] Lewin, "Action Research and Minority Problems," pp. 34–46.

Raymond Katzell, in the refinery action research project, suggested three types of situations in which the research consultant staff were providing data feedback to managers: the first situation was described as "adventitious," that is, the research group happened to have already collected data that turned out to be quite useful to someone at a later time; the second situation represented data collection on a refinery-wide basis of a preplanned, systematic nature, that is, a periodic pulse taking of the organization; the third situation was to work intensively with a small "demonstration" group, continuously collecting data on all sorts of topics and feeding them back to the group as they were needed.[22] The second situation is often found in programs involving surveys taken, say, annually. In this situation it is possible to measure changes in various parts of the organization over time. The third situation is also found in organization development programs where a team of consultants has time and energy to spend on researching the consequences of behaviors within a small group with whom they are working intensively.

Chein, Cook, and Harding enumerate four varieties of action research —diagnostic, participant, empirical, and experimental.[23] In diagnostic action research, the scientist enters a problem situation, diagnoses it, and makes recommendations for remedial treatment to the client. The recommendations are intuitively derived, not pretested, and usually come from the scientist's experience or knowledge. Often the recommendations are not put into effect by the client group. This gave rise to a second kind of action research, participant action research, in which the people who are to take action are involved in the entire research and action process from the beginning. This involvement both facilitates a carrying out of the actions once decided upon and keeps the recommended actions feasible and workable.

Empirical action research is that in which the actor keeps systematic, extensive records of what he did and what effects it had. This is similar to the practitioner's keeping a day-to-day diary. Limitations of this method are the difficulties found in any clinical data collecting: the actor may have too few experiences to draw from; he may encounter situations too divergent from one another to compare them; his situation may be unique and may not permit generalizations; he may lack objectivity in evaluating his own performance; and he may find difficulties inherent in being both researcher and change agent simultaneously.

A fourth variety of action research, the *experimental,* is controlled research on the relative effectiveness of various action techniques. There

    [22] Raymond Katzell, "Action Research Activities at One Refinery," in *An Action Research Program for Organization Improvement,* pp. 37–47.
    [23] Isadore Chein, Stuart Cook, and John Harding, "The Field of Action Research," *American Psychologist,* 3 (February 1948), 43–50.

is almost always more than one possible way of trying to accomplish something. The problem is to find which is the best. This is research *on* action in the strictest sense of both words.[24]

These authors indicate that experimental action research may make the greatest contribution to the advancement of scientific knowledge, but at the same time it is the most difficult to accomplish. The experimental nature of the research permits definitive testing of hypotheses, and that is good. Controlling conditions to the extent that the hypothesis is tested in exactly the same way over several situations is difficult to do, however, when clients want immediate answers to pressing problems. In situations like these, the research aspects of the project become subordinated to the problem-solving–remedial treatment requirements of the situation.

OD practitioners typically utilize participant action research and, occasionally, experimental action research. The participant model is highly congruent with current OD practices, and the experimental model, while being congruent, is simply harder to implement. In this regard, we maintain that the practice of organization development itself is in a sense a result of the experimental action research model, in that certain kinds of interventions (actions and hypotheses) were found to be effective by practitioners for achieving organization improvement and they were kept in the repertoire, while other interventions were found to be ineffective and were dropped from use.

WHEN AND HOW TO USE ACTION RESEARCH IN ORGANIZATION DEVELOPMENT

The OD process is basically an action research program in an organization designed to improve the functioning of that organization. Effective improvement programs almost always require a data base, that is, they rely on systematically obtained empirical facts for planning action, taking action, and evaluating action. Action research supplies an approach and a process for generating and utilizing information about the system itself that will provide a base for the action program.

The collaborative inquiry feature of action research suggests to practitioners and laymen alike the desirability for jointly determining central needs, critical problems, and hypotheses and actions. The potential experimental nature of actions inherent in action research provides a different "set" for managers as they try to solve problems, that is, viewing problems in cause-effect terms and viewing solutions to problems as

[24] *Ibid.,* p. 48.

only one action hypothesis from a range of several. The systematic collection of data about variables related to the organization's culture—which many laymen are only now coming to view as important determiners of performance—and testing the effects of managerial actions on these variables offer new tools for understanding organization dynamics. All these features fit with a program to improve the organization.

The natures of organization development and action research are very similar. They are both variants of applied behavioral science; they are both action oriented; they are both data based; they both call for close collaboration between insider and outsider; and they are both problem-solving social inventions. This is why we believe a sound organization development program rests on an action research model.

9

OD Interventions —
An Overview

The term *OD interventions* refers to the range of planned program-matic activities clients and consultants participate in during the course of an organization development program. These activities are designed to improve the organization's functioning through enabling organization members better to manage their team and organization culture. OD inter-ventions constitute the continually evolving technology—the methods and techniques—of the practice of organization development. Knowing the OD intervention armamentarium and knowing the rationale underlying the use of different interventions contributes substantially to understand-ing the philosophy, assumptions, nature, and processes of organization development. In these five chapters on interventions, we examine the techniques involved in applying behavioral science theory and practice to change and improve ongoing systems. In this chapter we look at issues, definitions, rationale, and several classificatory schemata related to inter-ventions. In chapters 10 through 13 we extend the discussion through an examination of the current inventory of OD interventions.

A DEFINITION OF OD INTERVENTIONS

The term OD interventions is currently being used in several different ways. On the one hand, this seems to be due to confusion and lack of definition; on the other hand, it is due to the fact that it quite accurately (if not precisely) refers to several orders of meaning in terms of level of abstraction. Is an OD intervention something that someone does to an organization, or is it something that is going on, that is, an activity? It is both. We prefer, however, that emphasis be placed on the activity nature of interventions; interventions are "things that happen," activities, in an organization's life.

One use of the term that is common with practitioners and laymen alike is that an intervention is something the outside consultant does to the client system. The major shortcomings of this definition are, first, that it does not provide for the client system doing something to itself without the assistance of an external, or even internal, consultant; and, second, it denies the joint collaboration that takes place between consultant and client. In OD programs, individuals and units within the organization often initiate activities designed to improve their functioning and do so on their own. These activities can clearly constitute OD interventions.

The term is often used to refer to any learning technique or method available to the practitioner. Thus, any one of the extant methods available, what Burke and Hornstein call "the social technology of OD,"[1] is an intervention according to this use. (These techniques are available both to the client system and to consultants.) This is probably the most common use, and it is an appropriate one. The technology of OD consists of educational activities, methods, and techniques; some "things to do" and "things to be sure not to do"; questionnaires, observation and interview schedules, and so forth. Any of these can appropriately be considered an intervention when it is used to bring about organization improvement.

Common usage also finds the term applied to the following different levels of activities:

A single task, say, a two-hour decision-making exercise

A sequence or series of related tasks designed around some theme or objective; for example, Beckhard's *confrontation meeting* is a series of tasks designed to surface an organization's major problems, determine the priorities for solving the problems, and assign responsibilities for actions [2]

A "family" of activities that are related but may be quite different; for example, the set of activities called team-building interventions are a wide variety of diverse activities all designed to improve a team's effectiveness as a unit, and the activities may relate to ways to perform the task better or to ways to improve the relations between the team members

The overall plan for relating and integrating the organization improvement activities that an organization might be engaged in over a period of years (this is generally referred to as the *intervention strategy,* the

---

[1] W. W. Burke and H. A. Hornstein, "Introduction" to "The Social Technology of Organization Development," prepublication copy, 1971, p. 1.

[2] Richard Beckhard, "The Confrontation Meeting," *Harvard Business Review,* 45 (March–April 1967), 149–53.

strategy of intervention, or the *OD strategy* of the organization development program)

All of these are correct uses of the term intervention, but they relate to different levels of abstraction and can thus be confusing at times.

Finally, to give our definition of the term: OD interventions are *sets of structured activities* in which selected organizational units (target groups or individuals) engage with a task or a sequence of tasks where the task goals are related directly or indirectly to organizational improvement. Interventions constitute the action thrust of organization development; they "make things happen" and are "what's happening."

The OD practitioner is a professional versed in the theory and practice of organization development. He brings four sets of attributes to the organizational setting: a set of values; a set of assumptions about man, organizations, and interpersonal relationships; a set of goals and objectives for himself and for the organization and its members; and a set of structured activities that are the *means* to implementing his values, assumptions, and goals. These activities are what we mean by the word *intervention.*

A BRIEF WORD ABOUT THE NATURE OF OD INTERVENTIONS

In the chapter on the nature of organization development, the characteristics, nature, and scope of OD interventions were discussed in relation to the OD process. Many of the characteristics ascribed to OD inhere also in OD interventions. The foundations and characteristics of the OD process are given there as follows: it is data based and experience based, with emphasis on action, diagnosis, and goal setting; it frequently utilizes work teams as target groups; it rests on a systems approach to organizations; it is a normative–re-educative strategy of changing; and it is an ongoing process. In this section we deal explicitly with OD interventions, covering some new materials and some old materials in a new way.

OD interventions are structured activities of selected target groups. Some "secrets" of OD are contained in this statement, because there are "better" ways and "worse" ways to structure activities in order for learning and change to take place. OD practitioners know how to structure activities in the "better" ways through attending to the following points:

Structure the activity so that the relevant people are there. The relevant people are those affected by the problem or the opportunity. For example, if the goal is improved team effectiveness, have the whole team engage in the activities. If the goal is improved relations between two separate work groups, have both work groups present. If the goal is to build some linkages with some special group, say, the industrial relations people, have them there and have the linking people from the home group there.

This preplanning of the group composition is a necessary feature of properly structuring the activity.

Structure the activity so that it is (1) problem oriented or opportunity oriented and (2) oriented to the problems and opportunities generated by the clients themselves. Solving problems and capitalizing on opportunities are involving, interesting, and enjoyable tasks for most people, whether it is due to a desire for competence or mastery (as suggested by White),[3] or a desire to achieve (as suggested by McClelland),[4] or whatever. This is especially true when the issues to be worked on have been defined by the client. There is built-in support and involvement, and there is a real payoff when clients are solving issues that they have stated have highest priority.

Structure the activity so that the goal is clear and the way to reach the goal is clear. Few things demotivate an individual as much as not knowing what he is working toward and not knowing how what he is doing contributes to goal attainment. Both of these points are part of structuring the activity properly. (Parenthetically, the goals will be important goals for the individuals if the second point above is followed.)

Structure the activity so that there is a high probability of successful goal attainment. Implicit in this point is the warning that expectations of practitioners and clients should be realistic. But more than that, manageable, attainable objectives once achieved produce feelings of success, competence, and potency for the people involved. This, in turn, raises aspiration levels and feelings of self- and group-worth. The task can still be hard, complicated, taxing—but it should be attainable. And if there is failure to accomplish the goal, the reasons for this should be clear so they can be avoided in the future.

Structure the activity so that it contains both experience-based learning and conceptual/cognitive/theoretical-based learning. New learnings gained through experience are made a permanent part of the individual's repertoire when they are augmented (and "cemented") through conceptual material that puts the experience into a broader framework of theory and behavior. Relating the experience to conceptual models, theories, and other experiences and beliefs helps the learning to become integrated for the individual.

Structure the climate of the activity so that individuals are "freed up" rather than anxious or defensive. Setting the climate of interventions so that people expect "to learn together" and "to look at practices in an experimenting way so that we can select better procedures" is what we mean by climate setting.

[3] R. W. White, "Motivation Reconsidered: The Concept of Competence," *Psychological Review*, 66 (1959), 297–334.

[4] D. C. McClelland, J. W. Atkinson, R. A. Clark, and E. L. Lowell, *The Achievement Motive* (New York: Appleton-Century-Crofts, 1953).

Structure the activity so that the participants learn both how to solve a particular problem and "learn how to learn" at the same time. This may mean scheduling in time for reflecting on the activity and teasing out learnings that occurred; it may mean devoting as much as half the activity to one focus and half to the other.

Structure the activity so that individuals can learn about both *task* and *process*. The task is what the group is working on, that is, the stated agenda items. The term process, as used here, refers to *how* the group is working and *what else is going on* as the task is being worked on. This includes the group's processes and dynamics, individual styles of interacting and behaving, etc. Learning to be skillful in working in both of these areas is a powerful tool. Activities structured to focus on both aspects result in learnings on both aspects.

Structure the activity so that individuals are engaged as whole persons, not segmented persons. This means that role demands, thoughts, beliefs, feelings, and strivings should all be called into play, not just one or two of these. Integrating disparate parts of individuals in an organizational world where differentiation in terms of role, feelings, thoughts is common probably enhances the individual's ability to cope and grow.

These features are integral characteristics of OD interventions and also of the practitioner's practice theory of organization development. Little attention is given to characteristics of structuring activities in the literature, but knowledge of them helps to take some of the mystery out of interventions and may also be helpful to people who are just beginning to practice OD.

A different approach to the nature of OD interventions is provided by Warren Bennis when he lists the major interventions in terms of their underlying themes.[5] He describes the following kinds of interventions: (1) *discrepancy intervention,* which calls attention to a contradiction in action or attitudes that then leads to exploration; (2) *theory intervention,* where behavioral science knowledge and theory are used to explain present behavior and assumptions underlying the behavior; (3) *procedural intervention,* which represents a critiquing of how something is being done to determine whether the best methods are being used; (4) *relationship intervention,* which focuses attention on interpersonal relationships (particularly those where there are strong negative feelings) and surfaces the issues for exploration and possible resolution; (5) *experimentation intervention,* in which two different action plans are tested for their consequences before a final decision on one is made; (6) *dilemma intervention,* in which an imposed or emergent dilemma is used to force close examination of the possible choices involved and the assumptions underlying them; (7) *perspective intervention,* which draws

[5] Warren Bennis, *Organization Development: Its Nature, Origins, and Prospects* (Reading, Mass.: Addison-Wesley Publishing Company, 1969), pp. 37–39. We have paraphrased and interpreted his list extensively.

attention away from immediate actions and demands and allows a look at historical background, context, and future objectives in order to assess whether or not the actions are "still on target"; (8) *organization structure intervention,* which calls for examination and evaluation of structural causes for organizational ineffectiveness; and (9) *cultural intervention,* which examines traditions, precedents, and practices—the fabric of the organization's culture—in a direct, focused approach.

Bennis' typology helps to provide a more thorough understanding of the nature of OD interventions while at the same time affording a classification scheme against which specific activities may be compared.

The nature of OD interventions—the structured activities designed to bring about system improvement—is complex and multifaceted. But certain themes recur in many interventions, the dynamics of the intervention process itself are becoming better understood, and there is a growing body of concepts that relates to the process of planned change. Considerable understanding of the nature of OD interventions is available to practitioners and clients alike as a result of this process. Just as an example, and to close this section on a serendipitous note: the *decision* to participate in an OD intervention may itself be a cause of organizational improvement. Just making the decision will signal to the members involved that the culture is changing, that new ideas and new ways of doing things are becoming more of a possibility and reality. This signal may itself cause changes in the direction of improvement. Our evaluation techniques and our theories of the intervention process are not sophisticated enough to handle such interactional complexities. That is for future practitioners at future times.

THE MAJOR FAMILIES OF OD INTERVENTIONS

Not all OD programs contain all the possible intervention activities, but a wide range of activities is available to the practitioner. As we see it, the following are the major "families" or types of OD interventions.

Diagnostic Activities: fact-finding activities designed to ascertain the state of the system, the status of a problem, the "way things are." Available methods range from projective devices like "build a collage that represents for you your place in this organization" to the more traditional data collection methods of interviews, questionnaires, surveys, and meetings.

Team-building Activities: activities designed to enhance the effective operation of system teams. They may relate to task issues, such as the way things are done, the needed skills to accomplish tasks, the resource allocations necessary for task accomplishment; or they may relate to the nature and quality of the relationships between the team members or between members and the leader. Again, a wide range of activities is possible. In addition, consideration is given to the different kinds of teams that may exist in the organization, such as formal work teams, temporary task force teams, and newly constituted teams.

Intergroup Activities: activities designed to improve effectiveness of interdependent groups. They focus on joint activities and the output of the groups considered as a single system rather than as two subsystems. When two groups are involved, the activities are generally designated intergroup or interface activities; when more than two groups are involved, the activities are often called *organizational mirroring*.

Survey-Feedback Activities: related to and similar to the diagnostic activities mentioned above in that they are a large component of those activities. However, they are important enough in their own right to be considered separately. These activities center around actively working the data produced by a survey and designing action plans based on the survey data.

Education and Training Activities: activities designed to improve skills, abilities, and knowledge of individuals. There are several activities available and several approaches possible. For example, the individual can be educated in isolation from his work group (say, in a T-group comprised of strangers), or he can be educated in relation to his work group (say, when a work team learns how better to manage interpersonal conflict). The activities may be directed toward technical skills required for effective task performance or may be directed toward improving interpersonal competence. The activities may be directed toward leadership issues, responsibilities and functions of group members, decision making, problem solving, goal setting and planning, etc.

Technostructural Activities: activities designed to improve the effectiveness of the technical or structural inputs and constraints affecting individuals or groups. The activities may take the form of (1) experimenting with new organization structures and evaluating their effectiveness in terms of specific goals, (2) devising new ways to bring technical resources to bear on problems.

Process Consultation Activities: activities on the part of the consultant "which help the client to perceive, understand, and act upon process events which occur in the client's environment." [6] These activities perhaps more accurately describe an approach, a consulting mode in which the client is given insight into the human processes in organizations and taught skills in diagnosing and managing them. Primary emphasis is on processes such as communications, leader and member roles in groups, problem solving and decision making, group norms and group growth, leadership and authority, and intergroup cooperation and competition. Emphasis is also placed upon learning how to diagnose and develop the necessary skills to be effective in dealing with these processes.

[6] E. H. Schein, *Process Consultation* (Reading, Mass.: Addison-Wesley Publishing Company, 1969), p. 9.

Grid Organization Development Activities: activities invented and franchised by Robert Blake and Jane Mouton, which comprise a six-phase change model involving the total organization.[7] Internal resources are developed to conduct most of the programs which may take from three to five years to complete. The model starts with upgrading individual managers' skills and leadership abilities, moves to team-improvement activities, then to intergroup relations activities. Later phases include corporate planning for improvement, developing implementation tactics, and concluding with an evaluation phase assessing change in the organization culture and looking toward future directions.

Third-Party Peacemaking Activities: activities conducted by a skilled consultant (the *third party*), which are designed to "help two members of an organization manage their interpersonal conflict."[8] They are based on confrontation tactics and an understanding of the processes involved in conflict and conflict resolution.

Coaching and Counseling Activities: activities that entail the consultant or other organization members working with individuals to help them (1) define learning goals; (2) learn how others see their behavior; (3) learn new modes of behavior to see if these help them to achieve their goals better. A central feature of this activity is the nonevaluative feedback given by others to an individual. A second feature is the joint exploration of alternative behaviors.

Life- and Career-Planning Activities: activities that enable individuals to focus on their life and career objectives and how they might go about achieving them. Structured activities lead to production of life and career inventories, discussions of goals and objectives, and assessment of capabilities, needed additional training, and areas of strength and deficiency.

Planning and Goal-Setting Activities: activities that include theory and experience in planning and goal setting, utilizing problem-solving models, planning paradigms, ideal organization vs. real organization "discrepancy" models, and the like. The goal of all of them is to improve these skills at the levels of the individual, group, and total organization.

Each of these families of interventions has many activities and exercises included in it. They all rely on inputs of both conceptual material and actual experience with the phenomenon being studied. Some of the families are directed toward specific targets, problems, or processes. For example, the team-building activities are specific to intact work teams, while the life-planning activities are directed to individuals, although this latter activity takes place in group settings. Some interven-

[7] R. R. Blake and J. S. Mouton, *Building a Dynamic Corporation through Organization Development* (Reading, Mass.: Addison-Wesley Publishing Company, 1969). This book is a treatise showing how grid organization development programs operate.

[8] R. W. Walton, *Interpersonal Peacemaking: Confrontation and Third-Party Consultation* (Reading, Mass.: Addison-Wesley Publishing Company, 1969), p. 1. This entire book is devoted to an explication of this specialized intervention technique.

tions are problem-specific: examples of this are the third-party peace-making activities and the goal-setting activities. Some activities are process-specific—that is, specific to selected processes: an example of this is the intergroup activities in which the processes involved in managing interfaces are explored.

Additional interventions used in OD exist and are discussed in the following chapters. Examples of important interventions that in themselves do not constitute a family are the confrontation meeting, sensitivity training, force field analysis, the role analysis technique (RAT), and so forth.

SOME CLASSIFICATION SCHEMATA FOR OD INTERVENTIONS

There are many possible ways to classify OD interventions. Several have already been given: the families of interventions represent one approach, and Bennis's types of interventions represent another approach. Our desire is to construct several classificatory schemata showing interventions from several perspectives. In this way, we can better accomplish our objective of examining OD from a kaleidoscopic rather than from a microscopic point of view.

One way to gain a perspective of OD interventions is to form a typology of interventions based on the following questions: (1) Is the intervention directed primarily toward individual learning, insight, and skill building or toward group learning? (2) Does the intervention focus on *task* or *process* issues? (Task is what is being done; process is how it is accomplished, including how people are relating to each other and what processes and dynamics are occurring.) A four-quadrant typology constructed by using these two questions is shown in Figure 9-1.

This classification scheme presents one approximation of the categories of various interventions; it is difficult to pinpoint the interventions precisely because a single intervention may have the attributes of more than one of the quadrants. Interventions simply are not mutually exclusive; there is great overlap of emphasis and the activity will frequently focus on, say, task at one time and process at a later time. Generally, however, the interventions may be viewed as belonging predominantly in the quadrant in which they are placed. It is thus possible to see that the interventions do differ from each other in terms of major emphasis.

Another way to view interventions is to see them as *designed to improve the effectiveness of a given organizational unit*. Given different organizational targets, what interventions are most commonly used to

Individual vs. Group Dimension

Focus on the Individual	Focus on the Group
Role analysis technique Education: technical skills; also decision making, problem solving, goal setting, and planning Career planning Grid OD phase 1 (see also below) Possibly job enrichment and Management by Objectives (MBO)	Technostructural changes Survey feedback (see also below) Confrontation meeting Team–building sessions Intergroup activities Grid OD phases 2, 3 (see also below)
Life planning Process consultation with coaching and counseling of individuals Education: group dynamics, planned change Stranger T–groups Third party peacemaking Grid OD phase 1	Survey feedback Team–building sessions Intergroup activities Process consultation Family T–group Grid OD phases 2,3

Task vs. Process Dimension — Focus on Task Issues / Focus on Process Issues

FIGURE 9-1

OD INTERVENTIONS CLASSIFIED BY TWO INDEPENDENT DIMENSIONS:
INDIVIDUAL-GROUP AND TASK-PROCESS

improve their effectiveness? This is shown in Figure 9-2. The elasticity of different interventions really becomes apparent in this figure, with many interventions being placed in several categories.

Examination of figures 9-1 and 9-2 reveals redundancy and overlap in that specific interventions and activities appear in several classification categories. This may be confusing to the reader who is new to the area of organization development, but it nevertheless reflects the use to which various interventions are put. Perhaps a positive feature of the redundancy is that it suggests patterns among the interventions that the practitioner knows but that may not be readily apparent to the layman. Some of these patterns become more apparent in Figure 9-3.

Another conceptual scheme for categorizing the OD interventions rests on an attempt to determine the central, probable underlying causal

Target Group	Types of Interventions
Interventions designed to improve the effectiveness of INDIVIDUALS	Life- and career-planning activities Role analysis technique Coaching and counseling T-group (sensitivity training) Education and training to increase skills, knowledge in the areas of technical task needs, relationship skills, process skills, decision making, problem solving, planning, goal setting skills Grid OD phase 1
Interventions designed to improve the effectiveness of DYADS/TRIADS	Process consultation Third-party peacemaking Grid OD phases 1, 2
Interventions designed to improve the effectiveness of TEAMS & GROUPS	Team building — Task directed — Process directed Family T-group Survey feedback Process consultation Role analysis technique "Start-up" team-building activities Education in decision making, problem solving, planning, goal setting in group settings
Interventions designed to improve the effectiveness of INTERGROUP RELATIONS	Intergroup activities — Process directed — Task directed Organizational mirroring (three or more groups) Technostructural interventions Process consultation Third-party peacemaking at group level Grid OD phase 3 Survey feedback
Interventions designed to improve the effectiveness of the TOTAL ORGANIZATION	Technostructural activities Confrontation meetings Strategic planning activities Grid OD phases 4, 5, 6 Survey feedback

FIGURE 9-2

TYPOLOGY OF OD INTERVENTIONS BASED ON TARGET GROUPS

mechanisms of the intervention, that is, the underlying dynamics of the intervention that probably are the cause of its efficacy. This scheme is more controversial: different authors might hypothesize different causal dynamics. This is due partly to the relative paucity of theory and research on interventions. But the practitioner chooses and categorizes interventions on the basis of assumed underlying dynamics of change and learning, and it might therefore be helpful to present a tentative classification scheme based on these mechanisms.

Several hypothesized causal mechanisms inherent in OD interventions may lead to change and learning. These causal mechanisms are found to greater and lesser degrees in different interventions, and it is probable that the efficacy of the different interventions therefore rests on different causes. Some features of different interventions that may be causally related to learning and change are presented below. These are used to construct Figure 9-3.

Feedback: This refers to learning new data about oneself, others, group processes, or organizational dynamics—data that one did not previously take active account of. Feedback refers to activities and processes that "reflect" or "mirror" an objective picture of the real world. Awareness of this "new information" may lead to change if the feedback is not too threatening.

Awareness of Changing Sociocultural Norms: Often people modify their behavior, attitudes, values, etc., when they become aware of changes in the norms that are helping to determine their behavior. Thus, awareness of new norms has change potential because the individual will adjust his behavior to bring it in line with the new norms. The awareness that "this is a new ball game" or that "we're now playing with a new set of rules" is here hypothesized to be a cause of changes in individual behavior.

Increased Interaction and Communication: Increasing interaction and communication between individuals and groups may in and of itself effect changes in attitudes and behavior. Homans, for example, suggests that increased interaction leads to increased positive sentiments.[9] Individuals and groups in isolation tend to develop "tunnel vision" or "autism," according to Murphy.[10] Increasing communication probably counteracts this tendency. Increased communication allows one to check his perceptions to see if they are socially validated and shared.

Confrontation: This term refers to surfacing and addressing differences in beliefs, feelings, attitudes, values, or norms to remove obstacles to effective interaction. Confrontation is a process that actively seeks to discern real differences that are "getting in the way," surface those issues, and work on the issues in a constructive way. Many obstacles to growth and learning exist; they continue to exist when they are not actively looked at and examined.

Education: This refers to activities designed to upgrade (1) knowledge and concepts, (2) outmoded beliefs and attitudes, (3) skills. In organization development the education may be directed toward increasing these three components in several content areas: task achievement, human and social relationships and behavior, organizational dynamics and processes, and processes of managing and directing change. Education has long been an accepted change technique.

[9] George C. Homans, *The Human Group* (New York: Harcourt, Brace & Co., 1950).

[10] G. Murphy, "The Freeing of Intelligence," *Psychological Bulletin,* 42 (1945), 1–19.

Some interventions emphasize one mechanism of change over others. A tentative typology based on these principal underlying change mechanisms is presented in Figure 9-3.

Hypothesized Change Mechanism	Interventions Based Primarily on the Change Mechanism
Feedback	Survey feedback T–group Process consultation Organization mirroring Grid OD instruments
Awareness of Changing Sociocultural Norms	Team building T–group Intergroup interface sessions First three phases of Grid OD
Increased Interaction and Communication	Survey feedback Intergroup interface sessions Third–party peacemaking Organizational mirroring Management by objectives Team building Technostructural changes
Confrontation and Working for Resolution of Differences	Third–party peacemaking Intergroup interface sessions Coaching and counseling individuals Confrontation meetings Organizational mirroring
Education through: (1) New Knowledge (2) Skill Practice	Career and life planning Team building Goal setting, decision making, problem solving, planning activities T–group Process consultation

FIGURE 9-3

INTERVENTION TYPOLOGY BASED
ON PRINCIPAL EMPHASIS OF INTERVENTION IN RELATION
TO DIFFERENT HYPOTHESIZED CHANGE MECHANISMS

This classification scheme, while differentiating between interventions, also shows the many multiple emphases that are found in many of the activities. We are only beginning to understand the underlying mechanisms of change in interventions. As that knowledge increases, greater precision in the selection of intervention activities will be possible.

The issue seems to be statable as follows: OD does in fact work; why it works is less well known and understood.

We find that another convenient classificatory scheme can be formed by categorizing OD interventions into those directed toward team improvement (Chapter 10), toward improving intergroup relations (Chapter 11), and toward the level of the total organization (Chapter 12) and those interventions that focus directly on personal, interpersonal, and group processes (Chapter 13). This scheme is similar to the typology based on target groups presented in Figure 9-2, but separates out the "process" interventions for special attention.

As a final note, in addition to knowledge about various interventions and knowledge about the appropriateness and timeliness of interventions, the OD practitioner is cognizant of the many dimensions inherent in each particular activity. Since an intervention contains the possibility for going in many directions, the practitioner attends to the range of alternatives in his own inputs. For example, in a team-building meeting, the practitioner will have various dimensions in his head that guide his inputs and contributions. These dimensions can be explained through looking at the questions the practitioner may be asking himself:

> We are dealing with individual behavior right now; how can this learning be translated to learning for the group?
>
> We are dealing with group phenomena right now; how can this learning be translated to learning for the individuals?
>
> We are focusing on task competencies and requirements; how do these relate to process issues and understanding of the group's dynamics?
>
> We have just learned about a phenomenon by experiencing it; what theoretical or conceptual material would augment this learning?
>
> We are dealing with issues and forces impinging on this group from outside the group; what activities must be designed to facilitate more appropriate handling of these interface issues?
>
> We are dealing with an old problem in a new way; does that signal a change in the sociocultural norms of this group, and are the members aware of it?
>
> We are diagnosing areas of interpersonal and intergroup conflict; what interventions are appropriate to deal with these issues?

SUMMARY

In this chapter we have taken an overview of OD interventions —the sets of structured activities in which selected organizational units (target groups or individuals) engage with a task or a sequence of tasks where task goals are related directly or indirectly to organizational improvement. Different definitions of OD interventions were discussed. The nature of interventions and several classifications of them were presented to gain a picture of interventions from several different perspectives. In the next several chapters OD interventions are described in greater detail in an inventory of most of the extant techniques and methods used in organization development.

10

a descriptive inventory of OD interventions
Team Interventions

In chapters 10 through 13 we examine in detail the intervention activities utilized to develop an organization. These activities are the techniques and methods designed to change the culture of the organization, move it from "where it is" to "where it wants to be," and generally enable the organization members to improve their practices so that they may better accomplish their goals.[1] The nature of these interventions and a preliminary look at the different types of methods have already been presented. In this chapter we want to present descriptions, goals, and mechanics of the various technical tools of OD practitioners that are directed toward improving the performance of intact work teams within the organization.

TEAM-BUILDING INTERVENTIONS

Probably the most important single group of interventions are the team-building activities the goals of which are the improvement and increased effectiveness of various teams within the organization. Some

[1] Detailed discussions of interventions can be found in several sources. The most complete treatment is given in J. K. Fordyce and R. Weil, *Managing WITH People: A Manager's Handbook of Organization Development Methods* (Reading, Mass.: Addison-Wesley Publishing Company, 1971). Additional sources are Richard Beckhard, *Organization Development: Strategies and Models* (Reading, Mass.: Addison-Wesley Publishing Company, 1969) and W. W. Burke and H. A. Hornstein, *The Social Technology of Organization Development* (Washington, D.C.: NTL Learning Resources Corporation, 1971).

interventions focus on the family group, an intact, permanent work team composed of a boss and his subordinates; while other interventions focus on special teams such as "start-up" teams, newly constituted teams due to mergers or organization structure changes, task forces, committees, and the like. The team-building interventions are typically directed toward four major substantive areas: diagnosis, task accomplishment, team relationships, and team and organization processes. These separate thrusts are diagramed in Figure 10-1.

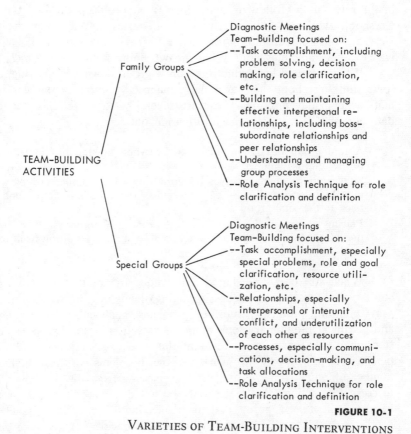

TEAM-BUILDING ACTIVITIES

Family Groups
Diagnostic Meetings
Team-Building focused on:
--Task accomplishment, including problem solving, decision making, role clarification, etc.
--Building and maintaining effective interpersonal relationships, including boss-subordinate relationships and peer relationships
--Understanding and managing group processes
--Role Analysis Technique for role clarification and definition

Special Groups
Diagnostic Meetings
Team-Building focused on:
--Task accomplishment, especially special problems, role and goal clarification, resource utilization, etc.
--Relationships, especially interpersonal or interunit conflict, and underutilization of each other as resources
--Processes, especially communications, decision-making, and task allocations
--Role Analysis Technique for role clarification and definition

FIGURE 10-1
VARIETIES OF TEAM-BUILDING INTERVENTIONS

Let us examine several of these interventions as they might be conducted with a family group. The major actors are a consultant, who is not a member of the group (the *third party*), the group leader, and the group members.

THE FAMILY GROUP DIAGNOSTIC MEETING

The purpose of the family group diagnostic meeting is to conduct a general critique of the performance of the group, that is, to take stock of "where we are going" and "how we are doing," and to surface and identify problems so that they may be worked on. Typically the leader and the consultant discuss the idea first, and if it appears that a genuine need of a diagnostic meeting exists, the idea is put to the group for their reactions. The leader may structure his testing for the group's reaction in the form of the following questions: What problems do we have that we should work on? How are we doing in regard to our assigned tasks? How are our relationships with each other? What opportunities should we be taking advantage of? What are we doing right and wrong?

If it is decided to conduct the family group diagnostic meeting, after some thinking about their own performance, the group assembles for a half-day or a day meeting. These are several ways to get the diagnostic data out, that is, to make the information public:

A total-group discussion involving everyone making his contributions to the total assemblage

Subgrouping, which involves breaking down into smaller groups where a more intensive discussion takes place, then the subgroups reporting back to the total group

Pairing of two individuals who interview each other or who simply discuss their ideas with each other, each pair then reporting back to the total group

When the data are shared throughout the group, the next steps consist of discussing the issues, grouping the issues in terms of themes (say, planning problems, interface problems, goal ambiguity problems), and getting a preliminary look at the next action steps. The next action steps may call for a family team-building meeting, may assign different persons to task groups to work on the problems, or may include a number of other strategies that involve moving from the diagnostic data to corrective action taking. It should be noted however that the primary focus of the family group diagnostic meeting is to surface issues and problems that should be worked on and to decide *how* to take action steps. Taking action is generally a postmeeting activity or an activity for subsequent team meetings.

The family group diagnostic meeting permits a group to critique itself and to identify its strengths and problem areas, and it allows everyone to participate in generating the necessary data. The data then form the basis for planning future actions. Such a meeting requires only a minimal expenditure of time. Semiannual diagnostic meetings afford an excellent method for staying on top of problems. A key secret to the success of a short diagnostic meeting is the realization by all participants that the meeting is for the purpose of identifying problems, not solving problems (an activity that may require considerably more expense of time and resources).

Diagnostic meetings for newly constituted groups, say, task forces or new teams resulting from mergers or acquisitions, are similar in form and function to the family group diagnostic meeting. These meetings may have to be held more frequently in order to stay ahead of the problems. Furthermore, linking diagnostic meetings with problem-solving sessions or team-building sessions may be indicated for newly constituted teams.

THE FAMILY GROUP TEAM-BUILDING MEETING

The family group team-building meeting has the goal of improving the team's effectiveness through better management of task demands, relationship demands, and group processes. It is an inward look by the team at its own performance, behavior, and culture for the purposes of dropping out dysfunctional behaviors and strengthening functional ones. The group critiques its performance, analyzes its way of doing things, and attempts to develop strategies to improve its operation. Sometimes the purpose of the meeting is a special agenda item, like developing the group's performance goals for the coming year. Often the purpose of the meeting is for the more general charge expressed in the question, How can we build ourselves into a better functioning team?

The family group team-building session is usually initiated by the supervisor in consultation with the third party. The idea is then tested for reactions against the group. (Conversely, the group may initiate the idea and take it to the boss if they sense pressing problems that need examination and solution.) A good length of time for the meeting is about three days. The session should be held away from the work place.

The usual practice for these sessions is to have the consultant interview each of the group members and the leader prior to the meeting, asking them what their problems are, how they think the group functions, and what obstacles are in the way of the group performing better. These interview data are categorized into themes by the consultant, and he presents the themes to the group at the beginning of the meeting. The group examines and discusses the issues, ranks them in terms of their importance, examines the underlying dynamics of the problems, begins to work on solutions to the problems, and establishes some action steps to bring about the changes deemed desirable. Often some kind of follow-up meeting is held to determine whether the action steps that were outlined were taken and to determine whether or not they had the desired effects. This is the flow of events for the family group team meeting. But let us look closer at the components.

The meeting may be called for a special purpose, such as a new member coming into the group, an organization structure change, or planning for the next year; or it may primarily be devoted to maintaining and managing the group's culture and processes. If it is a special purpose meeting, time should still be allocated to an examination and critique of the group's dynamics.

Several methods are available to generate data for the session. It is often desirable that the consultant interview the entire group, using an open-ended approach, such as "What things do you see getting in the way of this group being a better one?" This procedure introduces the consultant to the group members and allows him to assess commitment to the team-building session. The consultant decides in advance, and informs his interviewees, whether or not the information each gives to him will be considered public or confidential. There seem to be advantages and disadvantages to either approach. For example, if the information in the interviews is confidential, the interviewees may be more candid and open than they will be if they know the information is public. On the other hand, treating the information as public data helps to set a climate of openness, trust, and constructive problem solving. If the information is considered confidential, the consultant is careful to report his findings in a general way that does not reveal his sources of information. Other ways the agenda items for the meeting are developed are through such devices as the family group diagnostic meeting or through a survey.

The consultant presents his interview results in terms of themes. When everyone has understood the themes, these are ranked by the group in terms of their importance, and the most important ones form the agenda for the meeting. In the course of the meeting, much interpersonal and group process information will be generated, and that is examined too. The group thus works on two sets of items: the agenda items and the items that emerge from the interactions of the participants.

As important problems are discussed, alternatives for action are developed. Generally, the team-building meeting involves deciding on action steps for remedying problems and sets target dates for "*who* will do *what when*."

Significant variations of the team-building session entail devoting time to problem-solving methods, planning and goal-setting methods, conflict resolution techniques, and the like. These special activities are usually initiated in response to the needs demonstrated or stated by the group. The consultant often makes conceptual inputs (lectures or lecturettes), or he structures the situation so that a particular problem or process is focused on and highlighted. A wide variety of exercises may be interspersed into the three-day meeting, depending upon the problems identified and the group phenomena that emerge. (Illustration 4 in Chapter 1 describes some of these specialized activities that facilitate or build upon the emerging issues in a team-building meeting.)

Figure 10-1 suggests that team-building sessions may be directed toward problem solving for task accomplishment, examining and improving interpersonal relationships, or managing the group's culture and processes. It may be that one of these issues is the principal reason for holding the team-building meeting. For example, say the meeting is designed as a team problem-solving session to examine the impact on the team of a new function or task being added to the group's work requirements. Even in this case a portion of the session will probably be reserved for reflecting on *how* the team is solving its problems, that is, critiquing the group's processes. In this way the team becomes more effective at both the task level and the process level.

ROLE ANALYSIS TECHNIQUE (RAT) INTERVENTION

The role analysis technique intervention is designed to clarify role expectations and obligations of team members to improve team effectiveness. In organizations individuals fill different specialized roles in which they manifest certain behaviors. This division of labor and function facilitates organization performance. Often, however, the role incumbent may not have a clear idea of the behaviors expected of him by others, and equally often what he can expect from others to help him fulfill his role is not understood by him or by the others. Ishwar Dayal and John M. Thomas developed a technique for clarifying the roles of the top management of a new organization in India.[2] This technique is particularly applicable for new teams, but it may also be helpful in established teams where role ambiguity or confusion exists. The intervention is predicated on the belief that consensual determination of role requirements for team members, consisting of a joint building of the requirements by all concerned, leads to more mutually satisfactory and productive

[2] I. Dayal and J. M. Thomas, "Operation KPE: Developing a New Organization," *The Journal of Applied Behavioral Science*, 4, No. 4 (1968), 473–506. The present discussion is based on this article.

behavior. Dayal and Thomas call the activity the *role analysis technique.* In a structured series of steps role incumbents, in conjunction with team members, define and delineate role requirements. The role being defined is called the *focal role.* In a new organization, it may be desirable to conduct a role analysis for each of the major roles.

The first step consists of an analysis of the focal role initiated by the focal role individual. The role, its place in the organization, the rationale for its existence, and its place in achieving overall organization goals are examined along with the specific duties of the office. The specific duties and behaviors are listed on a chalkboard and are discussed by the entire team. Behaviors are added and deleted until the group and the role incumbent are satisfied that they have defined the role completely.

The second step examines the focal role incumbent's expectations of others. He lists his expectations of the other roles in the group that most affect his own role performance, and these expectations are discussed, modified, added to, and agreed upon by the entire group.

The third step consists of explicating others' expectations and desired behaviors of the focal role, that is, the members of the group describe what they want from and expect from the incumbent of the focal role. These expectations of others are discussed, modified, and agreed upon by the group and the focal role person.

Upon conclusion of this step, the focal role person assumes responsibility for making a written summary of the role as it has been defined; this is called a *role profile* and is derived from the results of the discussions in steps 1 through 3. Dayal and Thomas describe the role profile as follows: "This consists of (a) a set of activities classified as to the prescribed and discretionary elements of the role, (b) the obligation of the role to each role in its set, and (c) the expectations of this role from others in its set. Viewed in toto, this provides a comprehensive understanding of each individual's 'role space.' "[3]

The written role profile is briefly reviewed at the following meeting before another focal role is analyzed. The accepted role profile constitutes the role activities for the focal role person.

This intervention can be a nonthreatening activity with high payoff. Often the mutual demands, expectations, and obligations of interdependent team members have never been publicly examined. Each role incumbent wonders why the other guy is "not doing what he is supposed to," while in reality each is performing as he thinks he is supposed to. Collaborative role analysis and definition by the entire work group cannot only clarify who is to do what but ensure commitment to the role once it has been clarified.

From our experience, this procedure can be shortened if there

[3] *Ibid.,* p. 488.

is already high visibility and understanding of the current activities of various role incumbents. For example, if one of the problems facing an organization is confusion over the duties of the board of directors and the president or the executive director, the following sequence can be highly productive. (This technique was used in Illustration 4 of Chapter 1.) This would occur in a workshop setting involving the board, the president, and the key subordinates.

1. With the board listening, the president and his staff members discuss this question: "If the board were operating in an optimally effective way, what would they be doing?"
2. During this discussion, responses are made visible on a chalkboard or on large newsprint, and disagreements are recorded.
3. After forty-five minutes or so, the list is modified on the basis of general consensus of the total group.
4. The procedure is repeated, but this time the president listens while staff and board members discuss the question: "If the president were operating in an optimally effective way, what would he be doing?" Again, responses are made visible during the discussion. The president responds, and then there is an attempt at consensus.

As with the longer technique, this procedure helps clarify role expectations and obligations and frequently leads to some significant shifts in the whole network of activities of the management group, including the board. For example, we have seen this procedure result in boards shifting their activities almost exclusively to policy determination, pulling away from previously dysfunctional tinkering with day-to-day operating problems, and delegating operations to the president and the staff.

CONCLUDING COMMENTS

Collaborative management of the work team culture is a fundamental emphasis of organization development programs. This reflects the assumption that in today's organizations much of the work is accomplished directly or indirectly through teams. This also reflects the assumption that the work team culture exerts a significant influence on the individual's behavior. Usually, the technology and the theory for understanding and improving team processes come from the laboratory-training movement coupled with research in the area of group dynamics. An appreciation of the importance of the formal work team as a determinant of individual behavior and sentiments has come from cultural anthropology, sociology, organization theory, and social psychology. The interventions to be described in Chapter 13 are closely related to the activities found in team-building, team diagnosis, and role analysis interventions. Those interventions are more narrowly focused, but they also utilize the medium of the small group.

It is probable that if it were not for the interventions directed to improving intergroup relations (see Chapter 11) or interventions directed to improving the total organization (see Chapter 12), there would not be such a discipline as OD today; there would instead only be an expanded "small-group" discipline. We want to underscore that while the small group or team is an entry point in most OD strategies, and while ongoing attention to team effectiveness is a *sine qua non* for successful OD efforts, achieving total organizational improvement is possible only by going beyond the level of the team.

11

a descriptive inventory of OD interventions
Intergroup Interventions

When there is tension, conflict, or competition between groups some very predictable things happen: each group sees the other group as an "enemy" rather than as a neutral object; each group describes the other group in terms of negative stereotypes; interaction and communication between the two groups decrease, cutting off feedback and data input between them; what intergroup communication and interaction does take place is typically distorted and inaccurate; each group begins to prize itself and its products more positively and to denigrate the other group and its products; each group believes and acts as thought it can do no wrong and the other group can do no right; under certain circumstances the groups may commit acts of sabotage (of various kinds) against the other group.[1] Most people are aware of the existence of considerable intergroup conflict in organizations, and most people are aware of the patterns of behavior of groups in conflict. But few people know ways to alleviate the conflict to avoid the consequences of the conflict.

Several strategies for reducing intergroup conflict have been identified in the literature. They include finding a "common enemy" (an outside object or group that both groups dislike, which brings the groups closer together); increasing the interaction and communication between the groups (increased interaction under favorable conditions tends to be

[1] Research evidence for these statements comes from the following sources: M. Sherif and Carolyn Sherif, *Groups in Harmony and Tension* (New York: Harper & Row, Publishers, 1953); and R. R. Blake and Jane S. Mouton, "Conformity, Resistance, and Conversion," in I. A. Berg and B. M. Bass, eds., *Conformity and Deviation* (New York: Harper & Row Publishers, 1961). For a succinct summary of this issue, see E. H. Schein, *Organizational Psychology* (Englewood Cliffs, N.J.: Prentice-Hall, Inc., 1965), Chap. 5.

associated with increased positive feelings and sentiments); finding a supraordinate goal (a goal that both groups desire to achieve but that neither can achieve without the help of the other); rotating the members of the groups; and instituting some forms of training.[2] Even knowing these strategies for reducing intergroup conflict may not be very helpful —the questions still remain, How can we *implement* conflict-reducing mechanisms? and How do we *begin*?

In this chapter we examine the technology that has been developed to reduce intergroup conflict and to enhance intergroup relations. Because of the magnitude of intergroup problems in organizations these interventions are very important ones. In addition, the development of techniques to improve subsystems larger than single teams marked a significant step toward being able to improve total systems.

INTERGROUP TEAM-BUILDING INTERVENTIONS

The focus of the team-building group of OD interventions is on improving intergroup relations. The goals of these activities are to increase communications and interactions between work-related groups, to reduce the amount of dysfunctional competition, and to replace a parochial independent point of view with an awareness of the necessity for inter-dependence of action calling on the best efforts of both groups. It is not uncommon for a significant amount of dysfunctional energy to be spent in competition, misunderstanding, miscommunication, and mis-perception between groups. Organizational reward structures often encourage such behavior through emphasis on unit goal attainment as contrasted with total-organization goal attainment. Organization development methods provide ways of increasing intergroup cooperation and communication, as we see in this series of interventions.

One set of activities developed by Blake, Shepard, and Mouton is widely applicable to situations where relations between groups are strained or overtly hostile.[3] The steps go something like this: [4]

Step 1.   The leaders of the two groups (or the total membership) meet with the consultant and are asked by him if they think the relations between the two groups can be better and are asked if they are willing

[2] Schein, *Organizational Psychology,* Chap. 5.

[3] R. R. Blake, H. A. Shepard, and J. S. Mouton, *Managing Intergroup Conflict in Industry* (Houston, Tex.: Gulf Publishing Company, 1965).

[4] This discussion is based on R. Beckhard, *Organization Development: Strategies and Models* (Reading, Mass.: Addison-Wesley Publishing Company, 1969), pp. 33–35.

to search for mechanisms or procedures that may improve intergroup relations. Their concurrence that they are willing to search for ameliorative mechanisms is all that they are asked to commit themselves to at that time. If they agree to do this, the following activities take place.

Step 2. The intergroup intervention per se begins now. The two groups meet in separate rooms and build two lists. In one list they give their thoughts, attitudes, feelings, and perceptions of the other group —what the other group is like, what it does that gets in their way, etc. In the second list the group tries to predict what the other group is saying about them in its list—that is, they try to anticipate what the other group dislikes about them, how the other groups sees them, etc. Both groups build these two lists.

Step 3. The two groups come together to share with each other the information on the lists. Group A reads its list of how it sees Group B and what it dislikes about Group B. Group B reads its list of how it sees Group A and what it dislikes about it. The consultant imposes the rule that there will be no discussion of the items in the lists and limits questions to clarifying the meaning of the lists only. Next, Group A reads its list of what it expected Group B would say about it, and Group B reads its list of what it thought Group A would say about it.

Step 4. The two groups return to their separate meeting places and are given two tasks. First, they react to and discuss what they have learned about themselves and the other group. It typically happens that many areas of disagreement and friction are discovered to rest on misperceptions and miscommunication; these are readily resolved through the information sharing of the lists. The differences between the two groups are seen not to be as great as was imagined, and the problems between them are seen to be fewer than imagined. After this discussion, the group is given a second task: to make a list of the priority issues that still need to be resolved between the two groups. This list is generally much smaller than the original list. Each group builds its list of these issues.

Step 5. The two groups come back together and share their lists with each other. After comparing their lists, they then together make one list containing the issues and problems that should be resolved. They set priorities on the items in terms of importance and immediacy. Together they generate action steps for resolving the issues and assign responsibilities for the actions. "Who will do what when" is agreed upon for the most important items. That concludes the intervention.

Step 6. As a follow-up to the intergroup team-building activity, it is usually desirable to have a meeting of the two groups or their leaders to determine whether the action steps have in fact occurred and to "take a quick reading" on how the groups are doing on their action plans. This insures that the momentum of the intergroup intervention is not lost.

This procedure can also be used with large groups drawn from two very large populations. For example, after an expression of interest by parole officers and police officers in improving mutual understanding and relationships, we spent an evening with the two groups in an exercise called Project Understanding. By coincidence, members of the two groups happened to be attending workshops the same week at the same conference center. We simply divided the two large populations into small groups and paired off these small groups and conducted an exercise almost identical to the above sequence. Tentative action recommendations were posted in the large general session room for informal perusal during a social activity which followed.

A slightly modified version of this procedure is presented by Fordyce and Weil based on their experiences at TRW Systems.[5] In this version, two groups who have decided to work on improving their intergroup relations come together for the intergroup team-building meeting and are separated into two meeting rooms. Each group is assigned the task of building three lists as follows:

A "positive feedback" list containing the things the group values and likes about the other group

A "bug" list containing the things the group does not like about the other group

An "empathy" list containing a prediction of what the other group is saying in its list.

The two groups come together, and spokesmen for the groups read their lists. Questions are limited to issues of clarification only; discussion of the items is disallowed.

At this point, instead of breaking into separate groups again, the total group together builds an agenda or a master list of the major problems and unresolved issues between the two groups. The issues are prioritized in terms of importance.

Subgroups are formed containing members from each group and are given the task of discussing and working on each item in the list. After adequate time for working on the agenda items, the subgroups all report back to the total group.

On the basis of the information from the subgroups, the work on

[5] This discussion is taken from J. K. Fordyce and R. Weil, *Managing with People* (Reading, Mass.: Addison-Wesley Publishing Company, 1971), pp. 124–30.

the issues that has been going on, and the total information shared by the two groups, the participants now build a list of action steps for improving intergroup relations and commit themselves to carrying out the actions. For each of the action steps, people are assigned specific responsibilities and an overall schedule of completion for the action steps is recorded.

We have found that it is possible to work simultaneously with *three* groups in these kinds of intergroup activities, without the participants (or the consultants) finding the procedure too confusing. For example, in working with the key people in one Indian tribal organization, we requested each of three groups to develop lists about the other two groups plus themselves and to share the results in the total group. More specifically, the tribal council (one of the three groups) was requested to develop the following lists:

I. How the tribal council sees the tribal staff
   A. Things we like about the tribal staff
   B. Concerns we have about the tribal staff
II. What we (the tribal council) predict the tribal staff will say about us
III. How the tribal council sees the Community Action Program (CAP) staff
   A. Things we like about the CAP staff
   B. Concerns we have about the CAP staff
IV. What we (the tribal council) predict the CAP staff will say about us.

Concurrently, the tribal staff and the CAP staff developed comparable lists reflecting their perceptions of the other two groups and their predictions of what would be said about them.

These kinds of activities have been found to bring about better intergroup relations. It has empirically been shown time and again, in diverse situations, that in a relatively short time period (say, a day) these structured intergroup activities can result in improved intergroup relations. The intergroup problems and frictions are decreased or resolved, and intergroup communication and interaction are increased.

ORGANIZATION MIRROR INTERVENTIONS

The *organization mirror* is a set of activities in which a particular organizational group, the host group, gets feedback from representatives from several other organizational groups about how it is perceived and regarded. This intervention is designed to improve the relationships between groups and increase the intergroup work effectiveness. It is different from the intergroup team-building intervention in that three or more groups are involved, representatives of other work-related groups typically participate rather than the full membership, and the focus is to assist the host unit that requested the meeting.[6]

The flow of events is as follows: an organizational unit that is experiencing difficulties with units to which it is work related may ask key people from those other units to come to a meeting to provide feedback on how they see the host unit. The consultant often interviews the people attending the meeting before the meeting takes place in order to get a sense of the problems and their magnitude, to prepare the participants, and to answer any questions that the participants may have.

After opening remarks by the manager of the host group, in which he sets the climate by stating that his group genuinely wants to hear how the unit is perceived, the consultant feeds back to the total group information from the interviews. The outsiders "fishbowl" to discuss and explore the data presented by the consultant. (A fishbowl is a group seating and talking configuration in which there is an inner circle of chairs for people who talk and an outside circle of observers and noninteractors.) The fishbowl allows the invited participants to talk about the host unit in a natural, uninterrupted way while the host group members listen and learn. Following this, the host group members fishbowl and talk about what they have heard, ask for any clarification, and generally seek to understand the information they have heard. There may at this point be a general discussion to ensure that everyone understands what is being said, but at this time the participants do not start to work on the problems that have been uncovered.

For actually working on the problems, subgroups composed of both host group members and invited participants are formed. The subgroups are asked to identify the most important changes that need to be made to improve the host unit's effectiveness. After the small groups have identified the key problems, the total group convenes to make a master list to work out specific action plans for bringing about the changes deemed most important. The total group hears a summary report from each subgroup. Action plans are firmed up; people are assigned to tasks; and target dates for completion are agreed upon. This concludes the organization mirror intervention, but a follow-up meeting to assess progress and to review action steps is generally recommended.

In a short period of time an organization can get the feedback it needs to improve its relations with significant work-related groups. The oganization mirror intervention provides this feedback effectively. It is imperative that following the meeting the host group in fact implement the action plans that were developed in the meeting.

---

[6] Fordyce and Weil, in *Managing with People,* discuss this intervention in detail (pp. 101–5). We believe this technique was developed by the OD practitioners at TRW Systems.

12

a descriptive inventory of OD interventions
Total Organizational Interventions

Some OD interventions are sufficiently comprehensive to be categorized as total organizational interventions. In increasing order of comprehensiveness are the *confrontation meeting, survey feedback,* and *grid OD*. The confrontation meeting has a total organization quality because it simultaneously involves all the managers of an organization. Survey feedback typically involves all the employees of an organization (or a major subdivision), as well as managers, and includes two major phases. Grid OD, seen in its entirety, can involve all employees at all levels and has several distinct phases spanning several years.

THE CONFRONTATION MEETING

The *confrontation meeting,* developed by Richard Beckhard, is a one-day meeting of the entire management of an organization in which they take a reading of their own organizational health.[1] In a series of activities, the management group generates information about its major problems, analyzes the underlying causes, develops action plans to correct the problems, and sets a schedule for completed remedial work. This intervention is an important one in organization development; it is a quick, simple, and reliable way to generate data about an organization and to set action plans for organizational improvement. Beckhard says of the confrontation meeting:

[1] Richard Beckhard, "The Confrontation Meeting," *Harvard Business Review,* 45 (March–April 1967), 149–55.

Experience shows that it is appropriate where:
—There is a need for the total management group to examine its own workings.
—Very limited time is available for the activity.
—Top management wishes to improve the conditions quickly.
—There is enough cohesion in the top team to ensure follow-up.
—There is real commitment to resolving the issues on the part of top management.
—The organization is experiencing, or has recently experienced, some major change.[2]

The steps involved in the confrontation meeting are as follows: [3]

Step 1.   Climate Setting (forty-five to sixty minutes). The top manager introduces the session by stating his goals for the meeting, citing the necessity for free and open discussion of issues and problems, and making it clear that individuals will not be punished for what they say. This is generally followed by an input from the consultant regarding the importance of communication within organizations, the practicability of organization problem solving, and the desirability of addressing and solving organizational problems.

Step 2.   Information Collecting (one hour). Small groups of seven or eight members are formed on the basis of heterogeneity of composition, that is, there is a maximum mixture of people from different functional areas and working situations on each team. The only rule is that bosses and subordinates not be put together on the same team. The top management group meets as a separate group during this time. The charge to all the groups is as follows:

> Think of yourself as an individual with needs and goals. Also think as a person concerned about the total organization. What are the obstacles, "demotivators," poor procedures or policies, unclear goals, or poor attitudes that exist today? What different conditions, if any, would make the organization more effective and make life in the organization better? [4]

The groups work on this task for an hour and recorder/reporters list the results of the discussion.

Step 3.   Information Sharing (one hour). Reporters from each small group report the group's complete findings to the total group and these are placed on newsprint on the walls. The total list of items is

[2] *Ibid.,* p. 150.
[3] This discussion represents paraphrasing, *ibid.,* p. 154.
[4] *Ibid.,* p. 154.

categorized, usually by the meeting leader, into a few major categories that may be based on type of problem (e.g., communications problems), type of relationship (e.g., troubles with top management), or type of area (e.g., problems with the accounting department).

Step 4. Priority Setting and Group Action Planning (one hour and fifteen minutes). This step typically follows a break during which the items from the lists are duplicated for distribution to everyone. In a fifteen-minute general session, the meeting leader goes through the list of items and puts a category assignment on each one so that everyone has his own copy of the categorized items. Next the participants form into functional, natural work teams reflecting the way they are organized in the organization. Each group is headed by the top manager in the group. The groups are asked to respond to a three-part charge, that is, to do three tasks. First, they are to identify and discuss the issues and problems related to their area, decide on the priorities of these problems, and determine early action steps to remedy the problems that they are prepared to commit themselves (in the total group) to work on. Second, they are asked to identify the problems they think should be the priority issues for top management. Third, they are to determine how they will communicate the results of the confrontation meeting to their subordinates. This completes the confrontation meeting for all the managers except for the top management group.

Step 5. Immediate Follow-up by Top Team (one to three hours). The top management team meets after the rest of the participants have left to plan first follow-up action steps and to determine what actions should be taken on the basis of what they have learned during the day. These follow-up action plans are communicated to the rest of the management group within several days.

Step 6. Progress Review (two hours). A follow-up meeting with the total management group is held four to six weeks later to report progress and to review the actions resulting from the confrontation meeting.

This is the flow of activities for the confrontation meeting. It is an excellent way to get fast results leading toward organization improvement. Beckhard believes that the confrontation meeting provides a quick and accurate means for diagnosing organizational health, promotes constructive problem identification and problem solving, enhances upward communication within the organization, and increases involvement and commitment to action on the part of the entire managerial group.[5] We agree with his assessment.

[5] *Ibid.,* p. 153.

SURVEY FEEDBACK

An important and widely used intervention for organization development rests on the process of systematically collecting data about the system and feeding back the data for individuals and groups at all levels of the organization to analyze, interpret the meaning of, and design corrective action steps upon. These activities—which have two major components, the use of an attitude survey and the use of workshops—are called *survey feedback.*

An attitude survey, if properly used, can be a powerful tool in organization improvement. Most attitude surveys are not used in an optimal way—at the maximum, most give top management some data for changing practices or provide an index against which to compare trends. At the minimum, they are filed away with little of consequence resulting. (See Figure 12-1 for a comparison of two approaches to the use of attitude surveys—the traditional approach and the survey feedback approach.) Symptomatic of the lack of knowledge about how to use surveys effectively is the fact that most textbooks on personnel management do not refer to systematic data feedback in connection with their use for organization improvement. Those texts that do comment on feedback do so in a most cursory way. For us, data collection is only part of the process; appropriate feedback is an equally significant aspect.

Research at the Institute for Social Research at the University of Michigan indicates that if the survey is to be optimally useful, the following steps must occur: [6]

Step 1.   Organization members at the top of the hierarchy are involved in the preliminary planning.

Step 2.   Data are collected from all organization members.

Step 3.   Data are fed back to the top executive team and then down through the hierarchy in functional teams. Mann refers to this as an "interlocking chain of conferences." [7]

Step 4.   Each superior presides at a meeting with his subordinates in which the data are discussed and in which (*a*) subordinates are asked to help interpret the data, (*b*) plans are made for making constructive changes, and (*c*) plans are made for the introduction of the data at the next lower level.

[6] Floyd C. Mann, "Studying and Creating Change," in W. G. Bennis, K. D. Benne, and R. Chin, *The Planning of Change* (New York: Holt, Rinehart & Winston, Inc., 1961), pp. 605–13.
    [7] *Ibid.,* p. 609.

	Traditional Approach	Survey Feedback or OD Approach
Data collected from:	Rank and file, and maybe foreman	Everyone in the system or sub-system
Data reported to:	Top management, department heads, and perhaps to employees through news-paper	Everyone who participated
Implications of data are worked on by:	Top management (maybe)	Everyone in work teams, with work-shops starting at the top (all superiors with their subordinates)
Third-party inter-vention strategy:	Design and administration of question-naire, develop-ment of a report	Obtaining concurrence on total strategy, design and admini-stration of questionnaire, de-sign of workshops, appropriate inter-ventions in work-shops
Action planning done by:	Top management only	Teams at all levels
Probable extent of change and improvement:	Low	High

FIGURE 12-1

TWO APPROACHES TO THE USE OF ATTITUDE SURVEYS

Step 5. Most feedback meetings include a consultant who has helped prepare the superior for the meeting and who serves as a resource person.

The conclusions regarding the usefulness of survey feedback grew out of a four-year program with a large organization. In the first phase, data were gathered from some eight thousand employees throughout the company (1948). Comparable data were gathered two years later (1950) from the eight accounting departments, involving eight hundred em-ployees and seventy-eight supervisors. In this second phase, four of the eight departments carried on feedback activities as described above; two departments served as control groups with nothing further done after one all-department meeting; and two departments were eliminated from the design because of changes in key personnel. Two years later (1952), another survey was made and the researchers found that "more significant positive changes occurred in employee attitudes and perceptions in the four experimental departments than in the two control departments." [8] In particular, important changes occurred relative to how employees felt about "(1) the kind of work they do (job interest, importance, and level of responsibility); (2) their supervisor (his ability to handle people, give recognition, direct their work, and represent them in handling complaints); (3) their progress in the company; and (4) their group's ability to get the job done." [9]

From our experience, feedback workshops take on many of the characteristics of team-building sessions but are less likely to deal with interpersonal matters. However, they frequently focus on leadership style or on matters pertaining to cooperation and teamwork. For example, the following two items were included in a questionnaire used by one of the authors:

Management side-steps or evades things which bother people on the job.	Strongly Agree	Agree	Undecided	Disagree	Strongly Disagree

There is good cooperation and team work in my work group.	Strongly Agree	Agree	Undecided	Disagree	Strongly Disagree

In this questionnaire, items were included pertaining to "Organizational Climate," "Pay and Benefits," "Relations with Other Units," "Communications," "Supervisor/Employee Relations," "Performance Counseling," "My Job," "Pressure of Work," "Management by Objectives," "Opportunities for Personal Growth and Advancement," and "Training."

This kind of attitude survey, coupled with a series of workshops involving work teams at successively lower levels of the organization, can be used to create action plans and change across a wide range of variables in the social, structural, goal, and task subsystems of an organization. We think this approach has exciting possibilities because, in the words of Baumgartel (also quoted in Chapter 3), *"it deals with the system of human relationships as a whole . . . and . . . it deals with each manager, supervisor, and employee in the context of his own job, his own problems, and his own work relationships."* [10] This is the thrust

[8] *Ibid.*, p. 611.

[9] *Ibid.*

[10] Howard Baumgartel, "Using Employee Questionnaire Results for Improving Organizations," *Kansas Business Review,* 12 (December 1959), 6.

that permeates most OD activities and is one of the dimensions that differentiates OD from traditional interventions in organizations.

GRID ORGANIZATION DEVELOPMENT

Perhaps the most thoroughgoing and systematic organization development program is that designed by Robert R. Blake and Jane S. Mouton, *Grid Organization Development*.[11] In a six-phase program lasting about three to five years, an organization can move systematically from the stage of examining managerial behavior and style to the development and implementation of an "ideal strategic corporate model." The program utilizes a considerable number of instruments, enabling individuals and groups to assess their own strengths and weaknesses; it focuses on skills, knowledge, and processes necessary for effectiveness at the individual, group, intergroup, and total-organization levels. The organizational program is conducted by internal members who have been pretrained in grid concepts.

Basic to the Grid OD program are the concepts and methods of the Managerial Grid, also developed by Blake and Mouton, a two-dimensional schematic for examining and improving the managerial practices of individual managers.[12] One dimension underlying this diagnostic questionnaire is "concern for people"; the other dimension is "concern for production." The most effective managers are those who score high on both of these dimensions—a 9,9 position. A 9,9 management style is described as follows: "Work accomplishment is from committed people; interdependence through a 'common stake' in organization purpose leads to relationships of trust and respect." [13]

The relation between the Managerial Grid diagnostic questionnaire and Grid OD is explained by Blake and Mouton: "The single most significant premise on which Grid Organization Development rests is that the 9,9 way of doing business is acknowledged universally by managers as the soundest way to manage to achieve excellence." [14] As used in the Grid OD process, the Managerial Grid questionnaire becomes the vehicle for individuals and groups to examine and explore their styles. The pay-

[11] R. R. Blake and J. S. Mouton, *Building a Dynamic Corporation through Grid Organization Development* (Reading, Mass.: Addison-Wesley Publishing Company, 1969).

[12] R. R. Blake and J. S. Mouton, *The Managerial Grid* (Houston, Tex.: Gulf Publishing Company, 1964).

[13] Blake and Mouton, *Building a Dynamic Corporation through Grid Organization Development,* p. 61.

[14] *Ibid.,* p. 63.

off comes with a collaborative decision and plans to modify prevailing practices.

Behavioral science concepts and rigorous business logic are combined in the Grid OD program's six phases. These phases are described as follows: [15]

Pre-Phase 1. Before an organization (usually a business corporation) begins a Grid Organization Development program, selected key managers who will later be instructors in the organization attend a Grid Seminar. In this week-long experience-based laboratory, managers learn about Grid concepts, assess their own styles using the Managerial Grid questionnaire and the two-dimensional schematic, develop team action skills, learn problem-solving and critiquing skills, work at improved communication skills, and learn to analyze the culture of a team and of an organization. Learning takes place through the use of instruments, study team projects which are judged for adequacy, critiquing of individual and team performance, and conceptual inputs.

After several managers have gone to a Grid Seminar, some might go on to advanced Grid courses for further exposure to the Grid OD approach. At a Grid Organization Development Seminar, participants are taught the materials involved in Phases 2–6. They both learn what the Grid OD program is all about and learn how to conduct it in their own company.

Another advanced course is the Instructor Development Seminar, in which participants actually learn to conduct an in-company Phase 1 Grid Seminar. Training these managers in the various seminars accomplishes two things: the managers learn how to conduct a Grid OD program in their own organization, and they can also evaluate the Grid approach to determine whether or not they think it is a good idea for their organization to embark on such a course of action.

If, at this point, the company decides to implement a Grid Organization Development program, it might conduct a *pilot* Phase 1 program for volunteer managers. If the result of this is a "go" signal, then Phase 1 begins.

Phase 1: The Managerial Grid. In this phase, a grid seminar, conducted by in-company managers, is given to all the managers of the organization. The focus of the training is similar to that described above: attention is given to assessing an individual's managerial styles; problem-solving, critiquing, and communication skills are practiced; the skills of synergistic teamwork are learned and practiced. In this phase, managers learn to become 9,9 managers.

[15] This discussion is based on Blake and Mouton, *Building a Dynamic Corporation through Grid Organization Development,* pp. 76–109.

Phase 2: Teamwork Development. The focus of this phase is work teams in the organization. The goal is *perfecting* teamwork in the organization through analysis of team culture, traditions, and the like; and also developing skills in planning, setting objectives, and problem solving. Additional aspects of this phase include feedback given to each manager about his individual and team behavior; this critique allows him to understand how others see his strengths and weaknesses in the team's working.

Working on teamwork is done in the context of actual work problems. The problems and issues dealt with are the real ones of the team. In the process of Phase 2, individuals learn how to study and manage the culture of their work teams.

Phase 3: Intergroup Development. The focus of this phase is intergroup relations, and the goal of this phase is to move groups from their ineffective, often win-lose *actual* ways of relating between groups toward an *ideal* model of intergroup relations. The dynamics of intergroup cooperation and competition are explored. Each group separately analyzes what an ideal relationship would be like; these are shared between groups. Action steps to move toward the ideal are developed and assigned to individuals. The phase thus includes building operational plans for moving the two groups from their actual state to an ideal state of intergroup relations.

The phase consists of teams convening, in twos, to work on the issues stated above. Not all teams would pair with all others; only teams that have particularly important interface relationships do so. Often only selected members of the teams take part in the exercises and activities. These are the people who are closely work related with the other team.

Phase 4: Developing an Ideal Strategic Corporate Model. In this phase, the focus shifts to corporate strategic planning, with the goals being to learn the concepts and the skills of corporate logic necessary to achieve corporate excellence. The top management group engages in the strategy-planning activities of this phase, although their plans and ideas are tested, evaluated, and critiqued in conjunction with other corporate members. The charge to the top management group is to design an ideal strategic corporate model that would define what the corporation would be like if it were truly excellent. Fact-finding, technical inputs, etc., may be contributed from all persons in the organization.

Using the comparisons of ideal corporate logic versus real corporate logic, the top management team is better able to recognize what aspects of the culture must be changed to achieve excellence.

In a process that may take up to a year, the top executives build the ideal strategic corporate model *for their particular organization.* This is the model used in the next phase.

Phase 5: Implementing the Ideal Strategic Model. In several different steps, the organization seeks to implement the model of corporate excellence developed in Phase 4. To execute the conversion to the ideal strategic model, the organization must be reorganized. Logical components of the corporation are designated (these might be profit centers, geographical locations, product lines, etc.). Each component appoints a planning team whose job is to examine every phase of the component's operation to see how the business may be moved more in line with the ideal model. Every concept of the ideal strategic corporate model is studied by the planning team for its implications for the component. In addition, a Phase 5 coordinator is appointed to act as a resource to the planning teams.

The planning teams thus conduct "conversion studies" to see how the components must change to fit the ideal strategic corporate model. An additional planning team is formed and given the charge of designing a headquarters that would operate effectively and yet keep overhead to a minimum. After the planning and assessment steps are completed, conversion of the organization to the ideal condition is implemented.

Phase 6: Systematic Critique. In this phase the results of the grid OD program, from pre-Phase 1 to post-Phase 5, are measured. Systematic critiquing, measuring, and evaluating lead to knowledge of what progress has been made, what barriers still exist and must be overcome, and what new opportunities have developed that may be exploited. This phase is begun after Phase 5 is going well and is beginning to convert the organization well along toward the ideal model. Taking stock of where the corporation has been, how far it has come, and where it currently is thus represents a "new beginning" from which to continue striving toward corporate excellence.

Grid organization development is an approach to organization improvement that is complete and systematic and difficult. Does it work? Blake, Mouton, Barnes, and Greiner evaluated a number of grid OD programs and found significant organizational improvements that showed up on "bottom-line" measures such as greater profits, lower costs, and less waste.[16] Managers themselves, when asked about their own effectiveness and that of their corporation, likewise, declared that changes for the better had resulted from the program.

[16] R. R. Blake, J. S. Mouton, L. B. Barnes, and L. E. Greiner, "Breakthrough in Organization Development," *Harvard Business Review,* 42 (November–December 1964), 133–55.

13

a descriptive inventory of OD interventions

Personal, Interpersonal, and Group Process Interventions

The activities described in this chapter are learning techniques directed toward individuals, dyads and triads, and groups. The central theme of the interventions is learning through an examination of underlying processes. In *process consultation,* an important genre of OD interventions, there is an almost exclusive focus on the diagnosis and management of personal, interpersonal, and group processes. Expertise in this area is essential for OD practitioners. *Third-party peacemaking* focuses on interpersonal conflict and the dynamics of cooperation and competition in sociations of two and three. Implementing interventions in this area requires considerable competence. *Sensitivity training,* the educational and social invention giving rise to the laboratory-training movement, typically yields learnings about self, interpersonal relations, and group dynamics. We view sensitivity training as an important, but not prepotent, OD intervention technique. Life- and career-planning interventions are less process oriented than the other interventions in this chapter and reflect more a systematic approach to a substantive area that has heretofore received little attention. While these planning activities are intended to enhance individual functioning, the setting is generally the small group.

The interventions discussed in this chapter are important ones. Depending on the overall OD strategy, not all of them might be used in a particular OD program, but understanding the activities, and understanding when they are appropriate, is necessary for client and consultant alike.

PROCESS CONSULTATION INTERVENTIONS

Process consultation (P–C) represents an approach or a method for intervening in an ongoing system. The crux of this approach is that a skilled third party (consultant) works with individuals and groups to help them learn about human and social processes and learn to solve problems that stem from process events. This approach has been around a long time; many practitioners operate from this stance. Recently Edgar Schein has pulled together the disparate practices and principles of process consultation in a comprehensive and coherent exposition.[1] In this book he also describes the role of P–C in organization development.

Process consultation consists of many different interventions; it is not any single thing the consultant does. The paramount goal of P–C is stated by Schein as follows:

> The job of the process consultant is to help the organization to solve its own problems by making it *aware of organizational processes,* of the consequences of these processes, and of the mechanisms by which they can be changed. The ultimate concern of the process consultant is the organization's capacity to do for itself what he has done for it. Where the standard consultant is more concerned about passing on his knowledge, the process consultant is concerned about passing on his skills and values.[2]

Some particularly important organizational processes are communications, the roles and functions of group members, group problem solving and decision making, group norms and group growth, leadership and authority, and intergroup cooperation and competition.[3] The P–C consultant works with the organization, typically in work teams, and helps them to develop the skills necessary to diagnose and solve the process problems that arise.

Schein describes the kinds of interventions he believes the process consultant should make:

1. Agenda-setting interventions, consisting of:
   —Questions which direct attention to interpersonal issues.
   —Process-analysis periods.
   —Agenda review and testing procedures.
   —Meetings devoted to interpersonal process.

[1] E. H. Schein, *Process Consultation: Its Role in Organization Development* (Reading, Mass.: Addison-Wesley Publishing Company, 1969). The discussion is based on this source.
[2] *Ibid.,* p. 135.
[3] *Ibid.,* p. 13.

—Conceptual inputs on interpersonal-process topics.
2. Feedback of observations or other data, consisting off:
—Feedback to groups during process analysis or regular work time.
—Feedback to individuals after meetings or after data-gathering.
3. Coaching or counseling of individuals [see discussion following].
4. Structural suggestions:
—Pertaining to group membership.
—Pertaining to communication or interaction patterns.
—Pertaining to allocation of work, assignment of responsibility, and lines of authority.[4]

In Schein's view, the process consultant would most often make interventions in that same order: agenda setting, feedback of observations or other data, counseling and coaching, and, least likely, structural suggestions. Specific recommendations for the solution of substantive problems are not listed because to Schein such interventions violate the underlying values of the P–C model in that the consultant is acting as an expert rather than as a resource.[5]

In *coaching and counseling interventions,* which may be considered either as a part of P–C or as a set of interventions in their own right, the consultant is placed in the role of responding to such questions from groups or individuals as "What do you think I should do in this instance in order to improve my performance?" "Now that I can see some areas for improvement, how do I go about changing my behavior?"

Schein sees the consultant's role in coaching and counseling situations to be the following: "The consultant's role then becomes one of adding alternatives to those already brought up by the client, and helping the client to analyze the costs and benefits of the various alternatives which have been mentioned." [6] Thus, the consultant, when counseling either individuals or groups, continues to maintain the posture that real improvement and change in behavior should be those decided upon by the client. The consultant serves to reflect or mirror accurate feedback, to listen to alternatives and suggest new ones (often through questions designed to expand the client's horizons), and to assist the client in evaluating alternatives for feasibility, relevance, and appropriateness.

The basic congruence between theories of counseling and the theory of process consultation is pointed out by Schein: "In both cases it is essential to help the client improve his ability to observe and process data about himself, to help him accept and learn from feedback and to

---

[4] *Ibid.,* pp. 102–3.
[5] *Ibid.,* p. 103.
[6] *Ibid.,* p. 116.

help him become an active participant with the counselor/consultant in identifying and solving his own problems." [7]

The process consultation model is very similar to team-building interventions and intergroup team-building interventions except that in P–C greater emphasis is placed on diagnosing and understanding process events. Furthermore, there is greater emphasis on the consultant being more nondirective and questioning as he gets the groups to solve their own problems.

THIRD-PARTY PEACEMAKING INTERVENTIONS

Third-party interventions into conflict situations have the potential to control (contain) the conflict or resolve it. R. E. Walton has presented a statement of theory and practice for third-party peacemaking interventions that is both important in its own right and important for its role in organization development.[8] His book is directed toward interpersonal conflict—understanding it and intervening in ways to control or resolve the conflict. This intervention technique is somewhat related to intergroup relations described in Chapter 11, but there are many unique aspects to conflict situations involving only two people. In this section, rather than describe specific interventions, we explicate some of the features of the theory presented by Walton.

A basic feature of third-party intervention is confrontation: the two principals must be willing to confront the fact that conflict exists and that it has consequences for the effectiveness of the two parties involved. The third party must know how, when, and where to utilize confrontation tactics that surface the conflict for examination.

The third party must be able to diagnose conflict situations, and Walton presents a diagnostic model of interpersonal conflict based on four basic elements: the conflict issues, the precipitating circumstances, the conflict-relevant acts of the principals, and the consequences of the conflict.[9] In addition, conflict is a cyclical process, and the cycles may be benevolent, malevolent, or self-maintaining. For accurate diagnoses it is particularly important to know the source of the conflict. Walton speaks to this issue:

A major distinction is drawn between substantive and emotional conflict. *Substantive issues* involve disagreements over policies and practices,

[7] *Ibid.*

[8] R. E. Walton, *Interpersonal Peacemaking: Confrontations and Third Party Consultation* (Reading, Mass.: Addison-Wesley Publishing Company, 1969).

[9] *Ibid.*, p. 71.

competitive bids for the same resources, and differing conceptions of roles and role relationships. *Emotional issues* involve negative feelings between the parties (e.g., anger, distrust, scorn, resentment, fear, rejection).[10]

This distinction is important for the third-party consultant in that substantive issues require problem-solving and bargaining behaviors between the principals, while emotional issues require restructuring perceptions and working through negative feelings.

Intervention tactics for the third party consist of structuring confrontation and dialogue between the principals. Many choice points exist for the consultant. Walton lists the ingredients of productive confrontation:

1. mutual positive motivation [both parties are disposed to attempt to resolve the conflict]
2. balance in the situational power of the two principals [power parity is most conducive to success]
3. synchronization of their confrontation efforts [initiatives and readiness to confront should occur in concert between the two parties]
4. appropriate pacing of the differentiation and integration phases of a dialogue [time must be allowed for working through of negative feelings and clarification of ambivalent or positive feelings]
5. conditions favoring openness in dialogue [norms supporting openness and reassurance for openness should be structured for the parties]
6. reliable communicative signs [making certain each can understand the other]
7. optimum tension in the situation [there should be moderate stress on the parties] [11]

Most of these ingredients are self-explanatory, but some elaboration may be helpful on the differentiation and integration phases. In the differentiation phase of conflict, the principals clarify the differences that divide them and sort out the negative feelings they have; in the integration phase, the principals seek to clarify their commonalities, the positive feelings or ambivalence that may exist, and the commonality of their goals.

The third party will intervene directly and indirectly in facilitating dialogue between the principals. Examples of direct interventions would be interviewing the principals before a confrontation meeting, helping to set the agenda, attending to the pace of the dialogue, and refereeing the interaction; examples of more subtle interventions of the third party

[10] *Ibid.*, p. 73.
[11] *Ibid.* This list is taken from page 94; our interpretation is shown in brackets; Walton's discussion of the list is on pages 94–115.

would be setting the meeting on neutral turf, setting time boundaries on the interaction, and the like.

Third-party intervention into interpersonal conflict situations requires a highly skilled professional or a highly skilled layman who understands the dynamics of conflict. This intervention group should not be undertaken by the novice in the human and social processes of organizations.

SENSITIVITY-TRAINING LABORATORIES

Sensitivity-training laboratories were a cornerstone of early organization development efforts. These are used less frequently now as interventions, but they are still an important part of OD techniques. The reduction in the use of sensitivity training (or T-groups, *T* for *training*) is not due to its lack of effectiveness or its appropriateness for OD, but rather more to its being supplanted by such interventions as team building and process consultation. T-groups are still an excellent learning and change intervention, particularly for the personal growth and development of the individual.

A T-group is an unstructured, agendaless group session for about ten to twelve members and a professional "trainer" who acts as catalyst and facilitator for the group. The data for discussion are the data provided by the interaction of the group members as they strive to create a viable society for themselves. Actions, reactions, interactions, and the concomitant feelings accompanying all of these are the data for the group. The group typically meets for three days up to two weeks. Conceptual material relating to interpersonal relations, individual personality theory, and group dynamics is a part of the program. But the main learning vehicle is the group experience.

Learnings derived from the T-group vary for different individuals, but they are usually described as learning to be more competent in interpersonal relationships, learning more about oneself as a person, learning how others react to one's behavior, and learning about the dynamics of group formation and group norms and group growth. Benne, Bradford, and Ronald Lippitt list the goals of the laboratory method as follows:

1. One hoped-for outcome for the participant is increased awareness of and sensitivity to emotional reactions and expression in himself and in others. . . .
2. Another desired objective is greater ability to perceive and to learn from the consequences of his actions through attention to feelings, his own and others'. Emphasis is placed on the development of sensitivity to

cues furnished by the behavior of others and ability to utilize "feedback" in understanding his own behaviors.

3. The staff also attempts to stimulate the clarification and development of personal values and goals consonant with a democratic and scientific approach to problems and personal decision and action. . . .

4. Another objective is the development of concepts and theoretical insights which will serve as tools in linking personal values, goals, and intentions to actions consistent with these inner factors and with the requirements of the situation. . . . One important source of valid concepts is the findings and methodologies of the behavioral sciences. . . .

5. All laboratory programs foster the achievement of behavioral effectiveness in transactions with one's environment. . . . The learning of concepts, the setting of goals, the clarification of values, and even the achievement of valid insight into self, are sometimes far ahead of the development of the performance skills necessary to expression in actual social transactions. For this reason laboratory programs normally focus on the development of behavioral skills to support better integrations of intentions and actions.[12]

The T-group is a powerful learning laboratory where individuals gain insights into the meaning and consequences of their own behaviors, the meaning and consequences of others' behaviors, and the dynamics and processes of group behavior. These insights are coupled with growth of skills in diagnosing and taking more effective interpersonal and group action. Thus, the T-group can give to individuals the basic skills necessary for more competent action taking in the organization.

Uses of T-groups in OD are varied, but they are particularly appropriate to introduce key members of the organization to group methods and they are appropriate to give a basic skill level relevant to group and individual dynamics to individuals. In addition, the T-group may be constituted in several different ways depending on the desired outcome. There are "cousin" laboratories consisting of people from the same organization but who do not have direct working relationships with each other and in fact may not know each other. A different configuration is the "cluster" lab consisting of persons from different parts of the organization similar to the cousin labs, but each group also has "clusters" of work-related people—a twelve-person group may have three separate groups of four persons each who are related in their work in the organization. Another possibility is the "family T-group" in which the intact work team undergoes a T-group experience together.[13] Finally,

[12] K. D. Benne, L. P. Bradford, and R. Lippitt, "The Laboratory Method," in L. P. Bradford, J. R. Gibb, and K. D. Benne, *T-Group Theory and Laboratory Method* (New York: John Wiley & Sons, Inc., 1964), pp. 15–44. This quotation, pp. 16–17.

[13] Based on discussions in J. K. Fordyce and R. Weil, *Managing with People* (Reading, Mass.: Addison-Wesley Publishing Company, 1971), pp. 109–13.

individuals from an organization may attend a "stranger" lab composed of people from other organizations.

Many people think that organization development means putting everyone in the organization through a T-group. This is not correct. The T-group is only one technique out of many available to the OD practitioner. And laboratory training, while appropriate in some situations, is not the basic thrust or modality of OD.

LIFE- AND CAREER-PLANNING INTERVENTIONS

Managing against objectives is important for individual effectiveness as well as for organizational effectiveness. A series of interventions focus on the life goals and the career goals of individual organization members in order that they may better exert control over their own destinies. The interventions focus on past, present, and future. The tasks are completed by individuals and then discussed in small groups. The sequence of steps enables individuals to come to grips with the following issues:

1. An assessment of life and career paths up to this point in time, noting highlights, particularly important events, choice points, strengths, and deficiencies.
2. A formulation of goals and objectives related to both desired life style and career path—these are future-oriented goals.
3. A realistic plan for achieving the goals and moving systematically toward goal accomplishment; that is, the goals are specified, action steps needed to reach the goals are determined, and a schedule of target dates is established for measuring progress.

Generally life planning and career planning are done concurrently because career planning is but one subset of life planning.

One series of life- and career-planning exercises is shown below. Herbert A. Shepard is generally acknowledged as the author and originator of these exercises, and the role of these interventions in organization development programs is due primarily to him.

Life-Goals Exercise

First Phase

1. Draw a straight horizontal line from left to right to represent your life span. The length should represent the totality of your experience and future expectations.
2. Indicate where you are now.
3. Prepare a life inventory of important "happenings" for you, including the following:

      a. Any peak experiences you have had.
      b. Things which you do well.
      c. Things which you do poorly.
      d. Things you would like to stop doing.
      e. Things you would like to learn to do well.
      f. Peak experiences you would like to have.
      g. Values (e.g., power, money, etc.) you want to achieve.
      h. Things you would like to start doing now.
  4. Discussions in subgroups.

Second Phase

1. Take 20 minutes to write your own obituary.
2. Form pairs. Take 20 minutes to write a eulogy for your partner.
3. Discussions in subgroups.[14]

Additional approaches exist to get the individual thinking about his life and career trajectory and to provide data that may be shared in small-group discussion. For example, the outline of activities suggested by Fordyce and Weil has the following steps: [15] First, individuals working in small groups are asked to make a "collage"—a symbolic representation of their lives constructed out of art materials, old magazines and newspapers, and the like; these are posted on the walls for later discussion. Second, individuals write two letters, the instructions for which are as follows:

> Now imagine that you have died ten years from now. Write a letter from one of your best friends to another good friend, telling about you and your life. What do you *want* him to be able to say about you? Next, imagine you have been killed in an auto accident next week. Now write a similar letter. What would he be likely to say about you? [16]

At this point, the group discusses the collages and letters of each individual, giving the individual the chance to get feedback from the rest of the group about their reactions and also allowing the group to learn more about each other. This third step of public sharing serves to prepare the members for the next step, consisting of building a "life inventory," similar to the one described above. Following the preparation of the life inventory, each individual prepares a career inventory by writing answers to questions like the following: What facets of work (my career up to this point) do I like most, least? What do I think are my best

[14] These are representative of the life-planning exercises used in NTL Institute programs for the training of OD practitioners.

[15] Based on a discussion in Fordyce and Weil, *Managing with People*, pp. 131–33.

[16] *Ibid.*, p. 131.

skills, abilities, and talents that I bring to the work situation? What kinds of rewards do I seek from my job—money, status, recognition, being a part of a team, etc.? What new career areas do I want to pursue? What new skills do I need to develop for the new career areas? These inventories are shared and discussed within the group. As a final step, individuals set down a plan of action steps for achieving the goals they have identified.

Life- and career-planning activities may take only a day; or sometimes an entire week can be spent generating data about oneself, analyzing the data both individually and in groups, and formulating clear goals and action plans for achieving them. These activities have great meaning for organization members and are particularly helpful for individuals who feel that they are in a rut, who are contemplating a career change, or who have seldom introspected about their own life style and career pattern.

CONCLUDING REMARKS

In chapters 10 through 13 we have looked at the range and scope of intervention techniques used to increase organizational effectiveness. This descriptive inventory of most of the current major intervention techniques not only should provide a grasp of the specific activities involved in OD but also should impart a clearer understanding of the nature of the OD process. The OD armamentarium contains structured activities designed to improve effectiveness at the individual level (coaching and counseling activities, third-party peacemaking activities when there is interpersonal conflict, life- and career-planning activities, and T-group activities); it contains activities directed toward increased team effectiveness (team-building activities, diagnostic family meetings, process consultation, the organization mirror, the role analysis technique); it contains interventions designed to increase intergroup effectiveness (the intergroup team-building sessions, the organization mirror); and it contains interventions designed to effect total organization change (survey-feedback activities, Grid OD, and the confrontation meeting).

When these interventions are based on appropriate diagnosis and pre-work, and utilized in a systematic, strategic fashion, they can assist the client organization in making significant improvements.

14

Conditions
for Optimal Success

We wish to conclude Part II with a discussion of the conditions contributing to optimal success in the organization development process. Theory, research, and experience suggest that successful organization development efforts tend to evolve in the ways we will describe, and they have certain distinguishing characteristics. Conversely, unsuccessful efforts tend to feature mistakes or inattention relative to some of these dimensions. Specifically, the following are the conditions and phases that we see as important to successful organization development efforts, which we will elaborate on in this chapter:

1. Perceptions of organizational problems by key people, and perceptions of the relevance of the behavioral sciences in solving these problems
2. The introduction into the system of a behavioral scientist-consultant
3. Initial top-level involvement, or at least support from a higher echelon with subsequent top management involvement
4. The operationalizing of the action research model
5. Early successes, with expansion of the effort stemming from these successes
6. An open, educational philosophy about the theory and the technology of OD
7. Acknowledgment of the congruency between OD and many previous effective management practices
8. Involvement of personnel and industrial people and congruency with personnel policy and practice
9. Development of internal OD resources
10. Effective management of the OD process
11. Monitoring the process and the measuring of results.

PERCEPTION OF ORGANIZATIONAL PROBLEMS BY KEY PEOPLE

Initially, in successful organization devolpment efforts there is strong pressure for improvement, at least on the top management of an organization or one of its subunits, from both inside and outside the organization. In short, the key people have a real sense of things not going as well as they could. This is one of the distinguishing characteristics of successful change efforts as identified by Greiner in his review of seventeen change efforts, of which he labeled eleven "successful" and six "less successful." [1]

> The organization, and especially top management, is under considerable external and internal pressure for improvement long before an explicit organization change is contemplated. Performance and/or morale are low. Top management seems to be groping for a solution to its problems.[2]

We believe, however, that successful OD efforts can emerge in organizations that are in less trouble than that suggested by the above quotation. From our experience, the important thing is a sense that things could be better. We think that an OD effort can play an important "tune-up" role for an organization.

INTRODUCTION OF AN EXTERNAL BEHAVIORAL SCIENTIST CONSULTANT

A second important condition in the early phases of an organization development effort is that an outside behavioral scientist-consultant is brought in for consultation with a top executive (or the top manager in a subdivision) to diagnose organizational problems. While we do not wish to understate the possibility of an internal person emerging in this role at the beginning, the instances are going to be few when a person with sufficient training, stature, and role congruency can assume a major change-agent role without outside help. The external person is freer of the cultural constraints of the organization, can take more risks to his own career, and may be more highly trained.

INITIAL TOP-LEVEL SUPPORT OR INVOLVEMENT

The successful OD effort, however, does not necessarily need to start at the top, although this is the ideal circumstance. The important

---

[1] Larry E. Greiner, "Patterns of Organization Change," *Harvard Business Review*, 45 (May–June 1967), 119–30.

[2] *Ibid.*, p. 122.

condition is that an influential person at the top of some unit has insight into the potential applicability of the behavioral sciences to the solution of problems being faced by his unit and that he have some support from his superior in doing some preliminary exploring and experimenting. As Bennis states it, there needs to be "some kind of 'umbrella' protection from the next highest echelon. . ." [3]

As the OD effort proceeds within a unit, support from additional people outside that unit will become imperative. The surrounding informal social system will tend to become either resistive or supportive, and to accomplish the latter, key people in other units and key people higher in the organization will need to be kept informed of the objectives, activities, and general results of the efforts as they unfold. Again to quote Bennis: "It can be disastrous if the people most affected by organization development are not involved, informed, or even advised of the program." [4] Ultimately, this means there must be top management support and involvement.

The awareness of the applicability of behavioral sciences, of course, is a prerequisite for any OD effort, however long- or short-lived. This awareness could occur in one of many ways—for example, through reading, through attendance at a seminar or a workshop, through attendance in a laboratory-training session, through discussions with colleagues in a professional association, or through a dialogue with a consultant already doing some work for the organization. This awareness might be at either the cognitive or the experiential level, or both. For example, at the experiential level, a manager might have become aware of the possibility of improved staff meetings through experiencing the way a workshop was handled. More directly, an outside consultant might be brought in to conduct a short workshop or "microlab" in order to give the client system a brief acquaintanceship with the dynamics of, say, a team-building session. This, of course, presupposes somebody's prior awareness of the potential utility of such pre-work.

OPERATIONALIZING OF THE ACTION RESEARCH MODEL AND EARLY SUCCESSES

The consultant's initial efforts may be in response to a request for a more traditional intervention, such as an attitude survey or a review of personnel policies and practices. However, the consultant's approach, al-

---

[3] Warren Bennis, *Organization Development: Its Nature, Origins, and Prospects* (Reading, Mass.: Addison-Wesley Publishing Company, 1969), p. 57.
[4] *Ibid.,* p. 47.

though he may not use the terminology, quickly begins to take on an action research flavor with the concurrence and involvement of the key client.

Thus, a third important characteristic emerges. The action research model of preliminary diagnosis, data gathering, feedback, and action planning is operationalized, probably through a team-building session or through an attitude survey-feedback procedure. These initial interventions are found to be helpful, and additional requests for such assistance emerge laterally or from subordinate units within the organization. Greiner succinctly states the process:

> The new man, with top management support, engages several levels of the organization in collaborative, fact-finding, problem-solving discussions to identify and diagnose current organization problems.
>
> The solutions and decisions are developed, tested, and found creditable for solving problems on a small scale before an attempt is made to widen the scope of change to larger problems and the entire organization.
>
> The change effort spreads with each success experience, and as management support grows, it is gradually absorbed permanently into the organization's way of life.[5]

Thus, top management does not commit itself irrevocably to a five- or ten-year program but, in collaboration with the change agent, does make commitments relative to reasonably sized "chunks" of activities. Successes then lead to additional chunks, and the time perspective grows with the successes.

AN OPEN, EDUCATIONAL PHILOSOPHY ABOUT OD

We believe that it is extremely important to the long-range success of an OD effort that the mystery and mythology be minimized and that the technology be understood. This means that a high value must be placed on making the assumptions, theory, and practices underlying the OD effort open and visible. Most people do not wish to be manipulated or have things done to them, particularly in mysterious ways. The external change agent, and ultimately the internal resource people, will continuously need to assume the role of educators who make their knowledge accessible to all. The desired climate is one in which organizational members find that the options open to them have increased and find a high return from their own use of behavioral science knowledge. In short,

---

[5] Greiner, *Patterns of Organization Change,* p. 25.

a major emphasis in an OD program must be the opportunity for self-directed personal growth and increased effectiveness of individuals and groups.

ACKNOWLEDGMENT OF THE CONGRUENCY WITH PREVIOUS GOOD PRACTICE

Another quality of successful OD efforts is an open recognition by internal or external change agents that many OD or behavioral science assertions will be highly congruent with the better managerial practices already in existence in the organization. As a manager once expressed it, "I've been a very successful manager over the years and have worked hard and somewhat successfully to bring about a participative, open climate in my organization. Now people in the personnel department and the OD program are preaching the same stuff to me that I've been practicing for years, and I resent it." He also used the phrase "knights on white horses" with reference to the change agents. A successful OD effort needs such managers as allies and valuable resources, not as people who feel pushed around.

Issues about who is the expert versus who is not, and problems of semantics, tend to diminish as the successful OD effort matures. As the skills learned through various phases of the OD program begin to permeate the organizational culture, and as the action research model becomes internalized, the distinction between the change agents and the non–change agents, and between what is OD and what is effective management, becomes less and less distinct. It continues to be important, however, that organizational members have a common language and a common understanding relative to the basic underpinnings of OD—for example, action research, emphasis on work team culture, and so forth.

INVOLVEMENT OF PERSONNEL PEOPLE AND CONGRUENCY WITH PERSONNEL POLICY AND PRACTICE

In a company large enough to have a personnel and industrial relations executive, long-range successful OD activities require that this executive become heavily involved, or at a minimum, highly supportive. He is the one person in the organization whose main function is the design and implementation of human resource systems, and to whom such specialists as the wage and salary administrator, the training director, and the employment manager report.

We are obviously talking about a personnel–industrial relations role which is broader than collective bargaining. While OD efforts have considerable promise for shifting union-management relationships toward more of a problem-solving climate, the chief negotiator for the organization may be locked into a "win-lose" stance for a substantial period of time until the entire organizational climate shifts to a different mode. We do know of one labor relations director in a huge multinational company, however, whose breadth of vision and successful bargaining with the unions are beginning to result in a shift of climate in many of the company divisions toward a more participative and problem-solving leadership style relative to the total work force. On the labor relations side, the basic vehicles for this shift have been new labor contracts which have removed many traditional constraints on job boundaries and which now permit job enrichment activities. Additional features include wage increases tied to productivity and cost savings. On the supervision side in this company, the shift has come, in large part, through a variety of organization development activities, including team building, survey feedback, and management workshops.

Ultimately, it seems to us, it is essential that the entire personnel–industrial relations group, including people in salary administration, be involved in the organization development program. Since internal OD groups have such potential for acting as catalysts in rapid organizational change, the temptation is great, as we will discuss in Chapter 16, for them to see themselves as "good guys" and the other personnel people as "bad guys," or simply ineffective. Any conflicts between a separate organization group and the personnel and industrial relations groups should be faced and resolved. Such tensions can be the undoing of either program. Even in the absence of any serious conflict, the change agents in the organization development program clearly need the support of the other people who are heavily involved in human resources administration, and vice versa.

As we will discuss in more detail in Chapter 15, what is done in the OD program needs to be compatible with what is done in selection, promotion, salary administration, appraisal, and other formalized aspects of the human-social subsystem. For example, substantially improved performance on the part of individuals and groups is not likely to be sustained if financial and promotional rewards are not forthcoming. In short, management needs to have a "systems" point of view and to think through the interrelationships of the OD effort with the reward and staffing systems and the other aspects of the total human resources subsystem.

This congruency is largely built in at the Systems Group of TRW. The model there is to make the total personnel and industrial relations group an integral part of the OD program. People in such roles as employment manager and plant personnel director are also change agents. These specialists are supported by line managers who have demonstrated particular skill in consultation and by external OD consultants.[6]

DEVELOPMENT OF INTERNAL RESOURCES

The development of internal resources, as illustrated in the practices at TRW, is an important, if not inherent, feature of successful OD efforts. In the first place, continued growth in problem-solving skills, in effectiveness in managing meetings, and so forth, is synonymous with a successful OD effort. In other words, the organization incorporates and builds upon what it learns from the change agent, as suggested earlier in our comments about the open, educational nature of OD.

Ideally, as in the TRW model, both members of the personnel staff and a few line executives are trained to do some organization development work in conjunction with the external behavioral scientists. In a large organization, in particular, the demands for the help of change agents may soon exceed the immediate supply or may begin to cost substantially more than people employed full time by the organization. In a sense, then, the external change agent tries to reduce the organization's reliance on him by developing internal resources, both because of the growth and development inherent in successful OD and because of the cost or the availability of change agent skills. We do, however, see an important long-range role for the external consultant, as we will describe later.

EFFECTIVE MANAGEMENT OF THE OD PROCESS

A number of aspects relative to the management of the ongoing OD process need careful attention if the program is to meet with continuous success. These dimensions have to do with authenticity, consulting team and client-consultant relationships, coercion versus voluntarism, OD strategy, and coordination.

[6] See Sheldon A. Davis, "An Organic Problem-Solving Method of Organization Change," *Journal of Applied Behavioral Science,* 3,1 (1967), 3–21. See also "TRW Systems Group," in Gene Dalton, Paul Lawrence, and Larry Greiner, eds., *Organizational Change and Development* (Homewood, Ill.: Richard D. Irwin, Inc., 1970), pp. 126–31; and Harold M. F. Rush, *Behavioral Science Concepts and Management Application,* Studies in Personnel Policy, No. 216 (New York: National Industrial Conference Board, 1969), pp. 157–71.

Authenticity, in contrast to gamesmanship, is an extremely important characteristic of successful OD applications. The outside consultant, the internal coordinator, or the key clients need to work together to check periodically on fears, threats, and anxieties centering around the OD effort. Such problems need to be confronted as they emerge, including those stemming from the promises of overzealous advocates.

Not only is the outside change agent needed for his skills, but the organization needs him to act as a "governor"—to keep the program focused on real problems and to urge authenticity in contrast to gamesmanship. For example, the danger always exists that the organization will begin to punish or reward involvement in group-process kinds of activities per se, or reward superficial lip service to OD values, rather than focus on performance. In this sense, the culture of the organization can begin to take on a cultish kind of behavior which may be out of joint with meeting its objectives. The consultant can, of course, become part of that problem; in this regard there is simply no substitute for professional competence and self-awareness.

In connection with cultlike behavior, coercion relative to such matters as openness, attendance at T-groups, and the like, can be highly dysfunctional. While it is difficult to draw a line between persuasion and coercion, OD consultants and top management should be aware of the serious consequences of the latter, particularly when real feelings about it are submerged and a perfunctory acquiescence occurs. What is happening under such conditions, of course, is that the informal system is no longer being managed collaboratively, behavior is not authentic, trust goes down, and communications become guarded. These are consequences diametrically opposed to the objectives of an organization development effort.

The problem of gamesmanship can partially be minimized if the OD consultants constantly work on their own effectiveness in interpersonal relationships and their diagnostic skills so they are not in a position of "do as I say, but not as I do." To elaborate further, from our experience it is imperative that any OD consulting teams, including both internal and external change agents, work intensively at their own team relationships. Lack of attention to their own team relationships and effectiveness will reduce their constructive impact on the broader organization.

Both consultant and client must work together to optimize their knowledge of the organization's evolving culture and to optimize their mutual personal growth. As the consultant needs to be concerned about the personal growth of the key client, so the client needs to be concerned about the growth of the consultant. For example, this means some investment on the part of the client to keep the consultant sufficiently tuned in to what is happening in the organization.

Successful OD efforts also require a strategy which can be articulated and made visible. While the overall strategy will evolve, the process can be facilitated by cognitive maps showing where groups have been in their learning experience, where they might go next, and so forth. For example, it can be helpful to realize that follow-up team-building sessions might occur once per year for the purpose of diagnosing and reviewing progress. It can be helpful to realize that, as trust levels go up, it might be productive to focus more intently on conflict reduction and on learning conflict-reducing techniques. Negatively speaking, the constructive gains of the initial OD efforts can be lost if there is no emerging plan relative to what OD means for the long range for both the total organization and its subunits.

Such a long-range strategy is one of the key features of the Grid OD approach as described in Chapter 12. The six phases are deliberately planned to build on each other and to give the effort direction and focus.

The OD strategy as it relates to management development and other programs needs to be planned and articulated. Similarly, there need to be guidelines for subsequent phases or expansion of the OD effort—who has access to the consultants, whether follow-up activities have higher priority than new efforts with new groups, and the like. These are real issues in managing the OD effort and must be faced.

Issues of coordination and control of the OD program also need to be resolved between the key internal OD coordinator, external consultants, and clients. This is particularly relevant to OD activities in large organizations. Lack of coordination can result in incongruous philosophies and practices resulting in dysfunctional tensions between people in different subunits or between OD specialists. For example, high emphasis on T-grouping by consultants in one department or division and a deliberate de-emphasis by consultants in another could interject an unnecessary debate into the system which might better have been worked out within the consulting staff. On the other hand, overcontrol by a central coordinator can choke off useful preliminary and follow-up activities between consultant and client. For example, barriers placed between the client and the consultant can turn an OD effort into a kind of "dog and pony show" in which the consultant displays his "tricks" during a team-building session but is prohibited from working with the client group in an ongoing way. In short, we are arguing for a consensual approach to OD strategy, but also for an open, ongoing kind of relationship between consultant and clients in various subunits. Stating the case even more positively, we recommend that the internal OD coordinator encourage a long-range, direct relationship between consultants and key clients in the subunits of the organization.

MONITORING THE PROCESS AND MEASURING RESULTS

Finally, successful OD efforts require the application of the action research model to the OD process itself. There needs to be continuous audit of the results, both in terms of checking on the evolution of attitudes about what is going on and in terms of the extent to which problems that were identified at the outset by the key clients are being solved through the process.

The president and the "line" executives of the organization will evaluate the success of the OD effort in terms of the extent to which it assists the organization in meeting its human and economic objectives. For example, marked improvements on various indexes from one plant, one division, one department, and so forth, will be important indicators of program success. Because of other conditions that will be operating simultaneously, however, the demonstration of cause-and-effect relationships is going to be exceedingly difficult. In fact, both measurement and interpretation are going to be difficult.

We believe, however, that a substantial contribution has been made by University of Michigan people and others both to the data-gathering phase of the OD process and to the measurement of the results of OD efforts. In particular, we would draw attention to questionnaires like Likert's "Profile of Organizational Characteristics"[7] and to their applicability in measuring changes stemming from an OD program. Likert's "Profile," a questionnaire which asks respondents to comment on a variety of organizational dimensions, including leadership, communications, and decision making, essentially taps what Likert calls "causal variables" (e.g., pressure for results) and "intervening variables" (e.g., attitudes toward supervision, height of performance goals, and extent of cooperation).[8] This questionnaire, for example, was used at the Weldon Company to measure changes over a two-year period during a major organization development effort. These changes, in turn, were then related to productivity measures and other "end result" variables.[9]

At a less ambitious level, systematic interviewing or questionnaire polling of participants two or three months after a team-building session could be invaluable for justification of the effort or the modifications in the OD program. We think anecdotal evidence, both positive and

[7] Rensis Likert, *The Human Organization: Its Management and Value* (New York: McGraw-Hill Book Company, 1967), pp. 197–211.

[8] *Ibid.*, p. 76.

[9] *Ibid.*, pp. 29–40. See also Alfred J. Marrow, David G. Bowers, and Stanley E. Seashore, *Management by Participation* (New York: Harper & Row, Publishers, 1967).

negative, is also very useful. The informed judgment of participating managers, in particular, is extremely important. For example, we recently asked a vice-president in charge of a large operating division of a corporation if the team-building sessions and the OD effort in his division had been useful. His response: "You bet. Now we tell it like it is." This kind of data, supplemented by a more systematic collection of data, can be invaluable in diagnosing the utility and the strength and weakness of the OD effort.

Some Key Considerations and Issues

system ramifications
consultant-client relationships
mechanistic and organic systems
the future of OD

15

System Ramifications
and New Demands

In this chapter we will theorize about a few of the more salient ramifications of an organization development effort in terms of new demands which are likely to be made on the system. All parties concerned need to realize that if major organization improvements are to be made and sustained, managerial practices with respect to many subsystems will need to be modified if these practices are not already congruent with the OD effort.

FEEDBACK

Since more extensive data gathering, including making legitimate the areas of feelings and attitudes, is an integral part of an OD effort, people will need to learn how to give and manage feedback in such a way that it is not destructive and so that it is helpful. This means training in giving and receiving feedback, and it means paying attention to the gamut of feedback systems—all the way from interpersonal kinds of exchanges to subunit production or cost data and to organization-wide attitude surveys.

For example, at the interpersonal level, feedback tends to be the most constructive when a number of conditions are met, such as—

It is solicited.
It is fairly immediate after the event.
It is specific.
It is reported in terms of the consequences to the other party.
It is nonjudgmental in that it does not label the person "stupid," "worthless," and the like.

It is given when the basic motive is to improve the relationship (in contrast to a desire to punish, etc.).

It is given in private or in a supportive group atmosphere.

It is given in the spirit of mutual give-and-take.

At the level of subunit production or cost data, feedback is most helpful if it is reported—

Directly to the manager who can take remedial action, in contrast to top management or a staff department

Frequently enough so the manager can plan remedial action

Specifically, so that the manager can easily identify the problem area (this will usually mean that the respective manager will need to be involved in designing the reporting system).

In terms of attitude surveys, feedback tends to be the most constructive—

When it is sought by the unit involved

When unit data and aggregate organizational data are reported to the respective manager, but not data specific to other units (direct comparisons with peers tend to be highly threatening at first)

When managers plus their subordinates discuss the dynamics underlying the data with the help of a third party and make action plans (additional characteristics were discussed in Chapter 12).

In general, constructive feedback requires intervening at the appropriate depth, as defined in the previous chapter. In particular, this means that the feedback be *sought* and that it be *provided directly to the person or unit for appropriate action.*

JOB DESIGN

The design of jobs, that is, intervening in the task subsystem, has been a popular domain of the consultant since the days of Frederick Taylor and the "scientific management" movement. In recent years the thrust of that movement has been reversed, with considerable attention being paid to "job enlargement" and, most recently, to "job enrichment." Both *can be,* but are not necessarily, organization development interventions. Even some offshoots of scientific management, such as work simplification, can be congruent with OD and can be considered OD interventions.

For clarification, a distinction needs to be made between (*a*) job enrichment, or vertical job enlargement, and (*b*) horizontal job enlargement. The latter simply adds activities, such as soldering three connections instead of one, while job enrichment (vertical job enlargement) increases the proportion of planning and controlling components to the "doing" components of the job. (See Figure 15-1.[1])

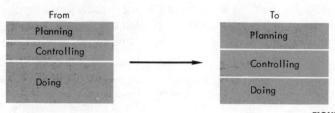

FIGURE 15-1

JOB ENRICHMENT
(VERTICAL JOB ENLARGEMENT)

Organization development activities incorporate some job enrichment features, since the process clearly includes some additional subordinate planning and controlling, particularly in group situations, that were not present before. Paradoxically, however, the "doing" aspects of jobs may become narrower or more routine. For example, an office work team may recommend and plan the elimination of some tasks that have become unnecessary, thus reducing the variety of tasks or even the complexity of the jobs.

At Texas Instruments, these kinds of shifts in the planning, controlling, and the doing aspects have occurred through the way the company has gone about the use of work simplification techniques. Work simplification at TI has involved supervisors and subordinates in problem-solving meetings in which they explore ways to eliminate unnecessary steps in production and to make tasks more efficient. In these meetings, work teams also decide who will perform which tasks and frequently divide up the work so that each member may have a mixture of challenging tasks along with the more repetitive tasks. And this process is supplemented by the work team participating in goal setting.[2]

[1] Figure 15-1 is adapted from M. Scott Myers, "Every Employee a Manager," *California Management Review*, 10 (Spring 1968), 9–20.

[2] See Harold M. F. Rush, *Behavioral Science Concepts and Management Application* (New York: National Industrial Conference Board Studies in Personnel Policy, No. 216, 1969), pp. 147–48. While this company has embarked on an extensive Managerial Grid OD program, the job enrichment activities seem to have preceded the more formalized OD effort; nevertheless, both applications at TI appear to be quite congruent. *Ibid.,* p. 146.

The point is that with a participative approach to job design in which the employee's advice is solicited relative to the design of his job and its relationship to a larger task subsystem, that is, in the use of the action research model and in the context of team diagnosis and planning, the effort is congruent with OD and can be considered an OD intervention. However, job enrichment activities are not necessarily congruent with organization development as we defined it in Chapter 2. Pertinent to that point, it is interesting that Herzberg and others, contrary to the practices at Texas Instruments cited above, almost seem to say that job enrichment *should* be imposed from topside:

> So far as the process of job enrichment itself is concerned, experimental constraints in the studies dictated that there could be no participation by jobholders themselves in deciding what changes were to be made in their jobs. The changes nevertheless seemed to be effective. On the other hand, when people were invited to participate—not in any of the reported studies—results were disappointing. In one case, for example, a group of personnel specialists suggested fewer than 30 fairly minor changes in their jobs, whereas their managers had compiled a list of over 100 much more substantial possibilities.
>
> It seems that employees themselves are not in a good position to test out the validity of the boundaries of their jobs. So long as the aim is not to measure experimentally the effects of job enrichment alone, there is undoubtedly benefit in the sharing of ideas. . . .[3]

Before we would conclude that Herzberg's experiments were really all that unilateral, however, we would want to know much more about the preliminary stages of his job enrichment programs. More joint diagnosis and joint planning may be involved than is immediately evident. In some organizations, task specialization may have proceeded so far that a joint diagnosis of the problem may have been occurring in the informal system for some time.

Our purpose here is not to quarrel with the successes or the failures of programs like job enrichment, but simply to state that we think that they may be sometimes highly congruent with organization development and sometimes highly different from OD and that they are sometimes OD interventions and sometimes not. In general, it depends upon what processes are used in their adoption and utilization.

CAREER DEVELOPMENT, TRAINING, AND STAFFING

If a major thrust of the OD process is to shift organization culture toward more honesty, openness, and increased personal development,

[3] William Paul, Keith Robertson, and Frederick Herzberg, "Job Enrichment Pays Off," *Harvard Business Review,* 47 (March–April 1969), 75.

the career and growth aspirations of all organization members must be an area of concern. These are matters of considerable interest to employees at all levels and will tend to become more openly talked about. This will probably mean paying more attention to advancement and transfer opportunities and will require more of a commitment of resources to training and management development. There might also be some commitment of resources to "life-planning" or "career-planning" workshops; a few organizations have experimented with such learning laboratories. Stranger T-group labs, of course, can be useful in the development of skills which will facilitate OD efforts. Technical courses might not be directly related to the OD process but could be very important in a systematic program of career development. These experiences, however, will tend to be more highly specific to individual and system needs than is the usual case, that is, more attention will be given to the diagnosis of training and development needs, with less reliance on "packaged" programs.

Another shift will probably occur. The climate could well shift from suppressing dialogue about the merits of leaving the organization toward openly facing the issue of internal versus external career opportunities. A likely outcome, as indicated above, will be more effort to increase opportunities for internal mobility. Ideally, new departments, divisions, or subsidiaries could be spawned through paying attention to the entrepreneurial and career aspirations of organizational members. Theoretically, the removal of arbitrary ceilings on responsibility will probably release a good deal of energy for constructive contribution within the system.

As an extension of changes in work group culture, the selection process will probably shift to a team approach in candidate evaluation, although we can see the possibility of higher trust levels permitting substantial delegation of this function, providing there is participation in the setting of criteria. Certainly, substantial attention will be paid to the process of introducing new people into the system if the staffing process is to be congruent with assumptions and values underlying the OD efforts. The experiment at Texas Instruments in the use of small-group discussions to reduce first-day anxieties is one example.[4]

It follows that exit from the organization is also likely to require more attention. It would clearly be inconsistent to be concerned about job and career needs up to retirement age and to ignore the dynamics of the inevitable separation. Resignations and involuntary separations are also occurrences to which an organization moving extensively into an organization development effort will want to pay considerable attention, both

---

[4] Carl R. Gomersall and M. Scott Myers, "Breakthrough in On-the-Job Training," *Harvard Business Review*, 94 (July–August 1966), 62–72.

after the fact and in a preventive way. For example, it is likely that inadequate performance would be faced more openly with the possibility of early correction, in contrast to unspoken resentments building up to a precipitous discharge.

TESTING AND THE ASSESSMENT CENTER CONCEPT

The developmental, organic philosophy inherent in the OD process creates a major dilemma relative to the use of psychological tests for selection purposes, particularly in the promotion system (see Chapter 17 for a discussion of "organic systems"). On the one hand, some tests, such as intelligence tests, can have sufficient validity in specific circumstances to warrant their use as one additional source of relevant data. On the other hand, tests can leave the candidate feeling subject to mysterious or arbitrary criteria or locked into his own personal characteristics which are not subject to modification.

The *assessment center* concept may provide some leads toward solving this dilemma. Briefly, companies using assessment centers typically give the candidate, usually a craftsman interested in promotion to foreman, an extensive battery of tests and involve him in an interview and group discussions and other group situations. Subsequently, line managers, who have been observing, make rankings of the relative performance of the candidates.[5] The ingredients that can shift the assessment center process from being strictly a matter of selection to one that is developmental are the dialogue that communicates the results to the candidate and the developmental opportunities that are subsequently provided. For example, if the assesment center highlights some deficiencies in group discussion, a center staff member can provide some feedback (ideally, requested by the candidate) and the organization may provide opportunities for developing additional skill. Then, too, the whole process of permitting candidates to apply for the assessment center experience and selecting some candidates for promotion tends to create an element of openness and mobility in the system which might not otherwise be there. One alternative, of course, is to hire from the outside.

To be truly developmental, however, the whole procedure must be based on great concern for the candidates and their careers, and the procedure must be highly open and explainable. Mystery needs to be

[5] For further discussion of the assessment center concept, see William C. Byhan, "Assessment Centers for Spotting Future Managers," *Harvard Business Review*, 48 (July–August 1970), 150–60; and Richard S. Campbell and Douglas W. Bray, "Assessment Centers: An Aid in Management Selection," *Personnel Administration*, 30 (March–April 1967), 7–13.

minimized in order to avoid distrust and to maximize learning. Furthermore, substantial attention must be paid to the nature of the dialogue that occurs between managers and subordinates. (Of considerable relevance are the conclusions from a study at General Electric to be discussed later.)

REWARDS

We think that any OD effort that increases the performance of organizational members and ignores the total pool of rewards accruing to the system will be self-defeating in the long run. In short, if there is a greatly increased sharing of responsibility and creativity in the attainment of organizational objectives and no proportionate sharing in the rewards, the OD effort will not be sustained. There is no reason to believe that the owners or the top managers of an organization have needs and motives that are drastically different from those of their subordinates, and a great deal of reason to believe that they are similar. The more organic and interdependent the system becomes, the more attention will need to be paid to congruity in the total reward system.

In both profit and nonprofit organizations, this means attention paid to rewards for both individual and team contribution. To place high value on team and interteam cooperation and then allocate rewards solely for individual efforts would clearly be dysfunctional. In a profit-oriented organization, a viable OD effort might eventually precipitate profit-sharing or stock ownership plans, or both.

Obviously, money is not the only reward accruing from the internal and external environments, and attention would also need to be paid to such matters as recognition and opportunities for interaction. For example, in a truly organic system the chief executive would no more jealously hoard all the emerging profits than he would attempt to isolate his subordinates from influential persons in the broader community or withhold recognition for high performance.

MBO AND APPRAISAL

To be congruent with the OD effort, the appraisal system needs to be both participative and transactional. By the latter we mean that an examination should be made of the major significant forces in the situation, including the superior's and the team's impact on the subordinate's performance, as well as an appraisal of the subordinate's performance.

Management-by-objectives (MBO) programs may include these qualities and in this context can be labeled OD interventions, but MBO programs can also be highly autocratic and nonparticipative. In their better forms, we see MBO programs as systems of joint target setting and performance review designed to increase the focus on objectives and to increase the frequency of problem-solving discussions between supervisors and subordinates, and ideally, within work teams. In their worst forms, MBO programs are unilateral, autocratic mechanisms designed to force compliance with a superior's directives.

Our hunch is that many MBO programs are imposed by line managers or personnel departments without much joint diagnosis. Furthermore, our hunch is that most MBO programs do not use a team approach, that they do not provide for sufficient acknowledgement of interdependency between jobs, and that rather than helping examine team culture, they tend to reinforce a one-to-one leadership style. Some of these are basic faults implicitly or explicitly pointed out by Harry Levinson in an article appropriately entitled "Management by Whose Objectives?" [6]

If a collaborative diagnosis indicates the desirability of an MBO program, then we think the implementation needs to include ingredients somewhat like the following in order to be developmental in contrast to dictatorial or punitive:

1. Real subordinate participation in setting goals
2. A team approach to reviewing targets and achievement
3. Problem-solving dialogues between team members and superiors and subordinates
4. A continuous helping relationship within teams and in superior-subordinate relationships
5. Attention to personal and career goals in a real effort to make these complementary to organizational goals
6. The development of trust between team members and skill in "process" matters

There is some research evidence to support these ingredients. Research at General Electric, for example, found that criticism by the superior tended to produce defensiveness and impaired performance, that goal setting and mutual goal setting between superior and subordinate were associated with improved performance, and that coaching needed to be a day-to-day activity.[7]

[6] Harry Levinson, "Management by Whose Objectives?," *Harvard Business Review,* 48 (July–August 1970), 125–34.
[7] H. H. Meyer, E. Kay, and J. R. P. French, Jr., "Split Roles in Performance Appraisal," *Harvard Business Review,* 43 (January–February 1956), 123–239.

ORGANIZATIONAL JUSTICE

A shift in team and organizational culture toward more openness and toward more mutual concern should, in large part, facilitate the airing of felt injustices. From our experience, this does occur and tends to happen in a more natural and less-threatening way. Grievances tend to be raised when they occur and are worked out quickly. (Parenthetically, this phenomenon plus others that tend to stem from OD efforts, from our observations, seemingly increases mental health. We see OD as a viable way of increasing mental health in an organization; many of its practices and underlying concepts are congruent with theory and clinical experience in counseling psychology, some aspects of psychiatry, and emerging community mental health programs.)

We are not recommending doing away with formalized appeal procedures, however, or what we would call *organizational due process.* We have defined the latter as consisting of "established procedures for handling complaints and grievances, protection against punitive action for using such established procedures, and careful, systematic, and thorough review of the substance of complaints and grievances." [8] We believe a formalized appeal system may be needed to protect individuals from gross anomalies in an organization's culture. For example, what if a norm begins to develop that says it is taboo ever to question the usefulness of any part of the OD effort? Or that subordinates should always be "open" no matter what the consequences might be, but that superiors may have hidden agendas? Or that talking about seniority is off limits even though employees feel deeply that length of service is a significant investment to be taken into account in job retention? Such an environment needs a formal appeal system. It is clearly consistent for a system that values openness to retain mechanisms that tend to protect openness.

MONETARY COSTS AND SKILL DEMANDS

The use of external and internal third parties in the role of change agents is obviously going to cost money. For an organization development effort to be successful, there needs to be a sustained commitment to the notion that the development of human resources is as important as the development of other kinds of resources. Symptomatic of lack of such

[8] Wendell French, *The Personnel Management Process,* 2nd ed. (Boston: Houghton Mifflin Company, 1970), p. 143.

commitment is the assumption that a one-shot team-building exercise will suffice to cure organizational problems. Experience shows that shifting to and maintaining the kind of culture we have been describing must be an ongoing process.

In addition, the costs in terms of effort and skill demands should not be ignored. In some ways, the environment we have been describing is more difficult and demanding than that found in more traditional organizational cultures. Team members, for example, no longer find it quite so comfortable to let the superior carry the responsibility for effective decision making or find it convenient to use scapegoats to rationalize why things went wrong. The newer culture is likely to include a commitment to examine all the forces bearing on a problem, including one's own impact.

Thus, while the newer culture may be, and usually is, more exciting and rewarding, it is likely to be more difficult and challenging as well. Implicit demands will be made upon organizational members constantly to improve their skills in managing the human-social subsystem as well as in technological or structural areas.

SUMMARY

A sustained, successful organization development effort will have extensive ramifications throughout the system. Attention will have to be paid to the design and quality of a wide range of feedback subsystems, to job design, to career development, training, and staffing, to monetary and nonmonetary rewards, to appraisal and performance review, to organizational justice, and to the monetary costs and skill demands involved. Programs like "job enrichment" and "management by objectives" can be considered OD interventions provided they meet a number of criteria, including joint diagnosis and a reinforcement of a team leadership style. In general, the administration and the underlying assumptions of a wide variety of organizational subsystems—the formal aspects of the human-social subsystem in particular—will need to be congruent with the OD effort if sustained organizational improvement is to occur.

16

Issues in Consultant-Client Relationships

A number of interrelated issues can arise in consultant-client relationships in organization development activities that need to be managed appropriately if adverse effects are to be avoided. These issues tend to center around whether a person or the system is the client, matters of trust, the nature of the consultant's expertise, the contract, diagnosis and appropriate interventions, the nature and depth of interventions, the consultant and consultant teams as models, action research as it relates to the OD process, and client dependency. There are no simple prescriptions for resolving these issues, but we do have some notions about them.

WHO IS THE CLIENT?

The question of who the client is quickly becomes an important issue in consultant-client relationships. We think a viable model is one in which, in the initial contact, a single manager is the client, but as trust and confidence develop between the key client and the consultant, both begin to view the manager's organization as the client. Ideally, this begins to occur in the first interview. Thus, the health and vitality of the various organizational subsystems, as well as the effectiveness and growth of all the individual members of the client system, clearly become the consultant's concern.

Although this is a controversial point, we find ourselves somewhat dubious about vague notions about the consultant representing the total organization when he is working with some subdivision of the total. To be effective he must have a relationship with, and be able to influence, the people in the system with which he engages. He cannot help those with

171

whom he does not interact—to attempt to do so would be working some unstated and mysterious agenda known only to himself. Or, if the consultant is carrying out some secret mandate of higher management, he is bound to fail in his relationships with his more immediate clients. The truth will eventually become apparent, and the consultant will be reduced to impotency. Even if he is open about some mandate from the top of the hierarchy, his efforts will tend to be minimized simply because he is carrying out an externally directed mission. Successful OD efforts are a process of mutual influence, not an imposed program from any direction.

The total system, however, will not be ignored in an effective consulting relationship with a subdivision. The effective consultant will have some ideas about what courses of action will be helpful and what will be dysfunctional relative to the total system, and he will express his sentiments—concerns, in particular—to his key client. The key client, moreover, will be the real expert about the broader system, and he and the consultant together will be looking for ways to improve the total. The real issue, then, is openness. If the client and the consultant are open with each other, the total system becomes a matter of joint concern.

THE TRUST ISSUE

A good deal of the interaction in early contacts between client and consultant is implicitly related to developing a relationship of mutual trust. For example, the key client may be fearful that things will get out of hand with an outsider intervening in the system. Subordinates may be concerned that they will be manipulated toward their superiors' goals with little attention given to their own. These kinds of concerns mean that the consultant will need to earn trust in these and other areas and that high trust will not be immediate.

Similarly, the consultant's trust of the client may be starting at neutral. He will be trying to understand the client's motives and will want to surface any that are partially hidden. For example, if the client has hopes that a team-building session will punish an inadequately performing subordinate, the consultant and the client will need to reassess the purposes of team building and examine whether or not that activity is the appropriate context for confronting the matter. On a positive note, the client may see OD as a means of increasing his own effectiveness and that of his subordinates, plus having hopes that a successful OD effort may bring considerable recognition from his superiors. Surfacing such motives and examining their implications for effective behavior will enhance trust between the consultant and the client and will help assure the eventual success of OD activities.

A related matter is the mystique surrounding organization development and related areas—laboratory training, in particular. In our judgment, the more that assumptions, theory, and technology are shared with the client and the client system, the more that trust develops and the more effective becomes the collaboration.

In this connection a common mistake is for external or internal consultants, in their enthusiasm, to be "selling" a kind of utopia instead of concentrating on helping clients with their problems. For example, they may be perceived as selling trust, openness, cooperation, and the like. While we believe these are good things, they are probably best worked on in the context of helping the client system solve those problems perceived as interfering with organizational effectiveness. In other words, being perceived as helpful enhances trust between client and consultant; conversely, selling philosophy may inhibit trust.

Trust and resistance problems also center around what we call the "good guy–bad guy syndrome." Internal or external OD consultants, through their enthusiasm for an exciting technology, may signal that they perceive themselves as the carriers of the message, that is, that they are "good guys," and implicitly that others are not, or at least are backward. This obviously creates all sorts of trust and resistance problems. People usually want to work collaboratively with others in the pursuit of common ends—but people also tend to resist being pushed around, under whatever banner. No one likes being put in the "bad guy" role, and we mistrust and resent those who seem to be doing that to us. This can be a trap not only for the consultant but also for the overly enthusiastic line manager.

THE NATURE OF THE CONSULTANT'S EXPERTISE

Partly because of the unfamiliarity with process consultation and other OD interventions, clients frequently try to put the consultant in the role of the expert on substantive content such as on personnel policy or organizational structure. We believe it is possible for the OD consultant to be an expert in the sense of sometimes presenting a range of options open to the client, but any extensive reliance on the traditional mode of consulting, that is, giving substantive advice, will tend to negate the OD consultant's effectiveness. He will need to resist the temptation of playing the content expert and will need to clarify his role with the client when this becomes an issue.

Lapsing into the expert role frequently stems from an overriding desire to please the client. The consultant wishes to maintain the relationship for a variety of reasons—professional, financial, or ego reasons—and naturally wishes to be perceived as competent. He therefore gets trapped into preparing reports or giving substantive advice, which, if more than minimal, will reduce his effectiveness.

There are at least two good reasons why the OD consultant should stay out of the expert role. The first is that a major objective of an OD effort is to help the client system to develop its own resources. The expert role creates a kind of dependency that typically does not lead to internal skill development. The second reason is that the expert role almost inevitably requires the consultant to defend his recommendations. With reference to an initial exploratory meeting, Schein refers to the danger of being "seduced into a selling role" and states that under such conditions "we are no longer exploring the problem." [1] In short, finding oneself in the expert role and defending one's advice tends to negate a collaborative, developmental approach to improving organizational processes.

An exception to the above is the desirability, or necessity of giving advice as to the design of a workshop, for example, or the design of a questionnaire. In the initial steps of the relationship, such advice is usually quite facilitating, providing the consultant is open to modifications of his suggestions by members of the client system. As Schein states it:

> the process consultant should not withhold his expertise on matters of the learning process itself; but he should be very careful not to confuse being an expert on *how to help an organization* to learn with being an expert on the *actual management problems* which the organization is trying to solve.[2]

OTHER DIMENSIONS OF THE INITIAL "CONTRACT"

Implicit in our discussion of the above issues is the issue of consultant and client formulating the "psychological contract." The resolution of such matters as who the client is, underlying concerns about how the OD effort might evolve, and whether or not the consultant will make substantive recommendations will have a major impact on subsequent events.

---

[1] Edgar H. Schein, *Process Consultation: Its Role in Organization Development* (Reading, Mass.: Addison-Wesley Publishing Company, 1969), p. 82.
[2] *Ibid.*, p. 120.

The more formal compensation aspects of the initial contract are also important and need to be confronted for the peace of mind of both client and consultant. We tend to prefer a verbal agreement as to an hourly or a daily fee, with no charge for an initial discussion—usually in our offices or over lunch, and sometimes over the telephone. Thereafter, we like to bill the client organization monthly for any time spent on the organization's behalf, although the approximate time amounts will be based on mutual agreement, with either party free to terminate the relationship should it not be mutually satisfactory. In the case of the internal OD consultant, the amount of time availability will be an important dimension.

Some consultants will charge for the preliminary exploratory discussions. Although we usually do not charge for such discussions, we find this a reasonable practice, since the key client frequently begins to develop new insight into the nature of the problem during the exploratory interviews.[3] Furthermore, in terms of the application of professional knowledge and skill, the initial meeting is as professionally demanding as the interventions that occur later as the OD effort unfolds.

DIAGNOSIS AND APPROPRIATE INTERVENTIONS

Another pitfall for the consultant is the convenience of applying intervention techniques with which he is familiar or which he particularly likes, but which may not square with a current diagnosis of unit problems. Thus, the consultant who is an effective T-group trainer may push participants in a team-building session into an intensive interpersonal laboratory session, while the more pressing issues may have to do with goal setting or role expectations. Or a consultant may rely heavily on a few instrumented techniques in his "bag of tricks" when the need for educational interventions may be minimal and the need for examining the manager's leadership style may be high.

We think a consultant should do what he can do, but his intervention should be reasonably appropriate to the diagnosis. The wider the range of interventions open to him, of course, the more he can be free to make a diagnosis unencumbered by anxieties about how to intervene. Inherent in making a perceptive diagnosis is an awareness of the complexity of and the interdependency of the various organizational subsystems.

[3] *Ibid.,* p. 82.

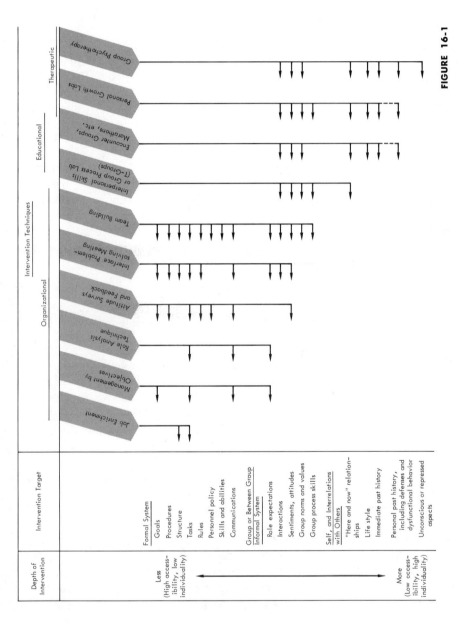

FIGURE 16-1

DEPTH OF VARIOUS GROUP OR ORGANIZATIONAL INTERVENTIONS

176

DEPTH OF INTERVENTION

In addition to the issue of selecting interventions from a range of interventions is the question of the depth of intervention. By *depth* we mean the extent to which the change target is the formal system, the informal system, or the self (see Figure 16-1 for a comparison of various group or organizational interventions in terms of depth [4]). In Harrison's terms, this continuum is based upon accessibility and individuality. By *accessibility* Harrison means the degree to which the data are more or less public versus being hidden or private, and the ease with which the intervention skills can be learned. By *individuality* is meant the closeness to the person's perceptions of self and the degree to which the effects of an intervention are in the individual in contrast to the organization. We are assuming that the closer one moves on this continuum to the sense of self, the more the inherent processes have to do with emotions, values, and hidden matters and, consequently, the more potent they are to do either good or harm. It requires a careful diagnosis to determine that these interventions are appropriate and relevant. If they are inappropriate they may be destructive or, at a minimum, will be unacceptable to the client or the client system.

To minimize these risks, Harrison suggests two criteria for determining the appropriate depth of intervention:

first, to *intervene at a level no deeper than that required to produce enduring solutions to the problems at hand;* and, second, to *intervene at a level no deeper than that at which the energy and resources of the client can be committed to problem solving and to change.* [5]

To Harrison, these criteria require that the consultant proceed no faster or deeper than the legitimation he obtains from the client system culture and that he stay at the level of consciously felt needs.[6] We think these are sound guidelines.

Harrison does recognize, however, and we agree, that the change agent is continuously confronted by the dilemma of whether to "lead and push, or to collaborate and follow." [7] Harrison's orientation is to the latter, but we are inclined to be slightly less conservative. We think that, to be effective the consultant needs occasionally but prudently

[4] This discussion and Figure 16-1 were stimulated by and draw upon Roger Harrison's essay, "Choosing the Depth of Organizational Intervention," *Journal of Applied Behavioral Science,* 6 (April–June 1970), 181–202.

[5] *Ibid.,* p. 201.

[6] *Ibid.,* pp. 198–99.

[7] *Ibid.,* p. 202.

to take minor risks in the direction of leading and pushing, but these risks should not be quantum jumps. As he develops expertise in diagnosis and in making interventions, the risks he tends to run are mainly the risks of a rejected suggestion. We do, however, agree with the essence of what Harrison is suggesting and agree with his criteria.

THE CONSULTANT AS A MODEL

Another important issue is whether or not the change agent is willing and able to practice what he preaches. In the area of feelings, for example, the consultant may be advocating a more open system in which feelings are considered legitimate and their expression important to effective problem solving while at the same time sitting on his own feelings about what is happening in the client system. In particular, this can be a frequent problem for the less-experienced change agent, and it usually has an impact on his feeling of competency: "If only I had said. . . ." The more he learns to be in touch with his own feelings, the more spontaneous he can be, and the more options are open to him. (This is one reason why we recommend extensive T-group experience for OD consultants.) However, the client system is not the appropriate ground for the consultant to work out the problems he brings with him. On the other hand, being too aloof emotionally will minimize his help to the client.

As another example of modeling behavior, the consultant needs to give out clear messages—that is, his words and his apparent feelings need to be congruent. He also needs to check on meanings, to suggest optional methods of solving problems, to encourage and support, to give feedback in constructive ways and to accept feedback, to help formulate issues, and to provide a spirit of inquiry.[8] We are not suggesting that he must be a paragon of virtue; rather, we are suggesting that to maximize his effectiveness he needs to continuously practice and develop the effective behaviors he wishes to instill in the client system.

THE CONSULTANT TEAM AS A MICROCOSM

The consultant–key client viewed as a team, or consultants working as a team, can profitably be viewed as a microcosm of the organization they are trying to create. In the first place, the consultant team needs to

[8] For a more extensive discussion of helpful consultant behaviors, see Charles K. Ferguson, "Concerning the Nature of Human Systems and the Consultant's Role," *Journal of Applied Behavioral Science*, 4 (April–June 1968), 179–93.

set an example of an effective unit if the team is to enhance its credibility. Second, change agents need the effectiveness that comes from continuous growth and renewal processes. And third, the quality of the interrelationships within the consulting team carries over directly into the quality of their diagnosis, their workshop or laboratory design, and their interventions. To be more explicit about the latter point, unresolved and growing conflict between two consultants can paralyze a workshop. Or simple lack of attention to team maintenance matters can produce morale problems which reduce spontaneity and creativity in planning sessions or in interacting with the client system.

ACTION RESEARCH AND THE OD PROCESS

A related issue is whether or not the OD process itself will be subject to the ongoing action research being experienced by the client system. The issue of congruency is, of course, important, but the viability of the OD effort and the effectiveness of the consultants may be at stake. Unless there are feedback loops relative to various interventions and stages in the OD process, the change agents and the organization will not learn how to make the future OD interventions more effective.

Feedback loops do not necessarily have to be complicated. Simple questionnaires or interviews can be very helpful. As an illustration, we recall having lunch with the key people who had been involved in a problem-solving workshop, and upon asking several questions about how things were going "back at the shop," we found that problems had emerged centering around who had been invited to attend the workshop and who had not. This feedback, at a minimum, has caused us to pay even more attention to pre-work and to helping workshop participants plan how to share effectively what has transpired with those not attending.

THE DEPENDENCY ISSUE

If the consultant is in the business of enhancing the client system's abilities in problem solving and renewal, then he is in the business of assisting the client to internalize skills and insights rather than to create a prolonged dependency relationship. This tends not to be much of an issue, however, if the consultant and the client can work out the expert versus facilitator issue described earlier and if the consultant subscribes to the notion that OD should be a shared technology. The facilitator role, we believe, creates less dependency and more client growth than the traditional consulting modes, and the notion of a shared technology leads to rapid learning on the part of the client.

The latter notion is congruent with Argyris's admonition that if the consultant intervention is to be helpful in an ongoing sense, it is imperative for the client to have "free, informed choice." And to have this free choice, it is necessary for "the client to have a cognitive map of what he wishes to do." [9] Thus, the consultant will have to be quite open about such matters as the objectives of the various interventions he makes and about the sequence of planned events. He should continuously be in the role of the educator as he intervenes in the system.

An issue of personal importance to the consultant is the dilemma of his working to increase the resourcefulness of the client versus his wanting to remain involved, to feel needed, and to feel competent. We think there is a satisfactory solution to this dilemma. A good case can be made, we believe, for a gradual reduction in external consultant use as an OD effort reaches maturity. In a large organization, one or more key consultants may be retained in an ongoing relationship, but with less frequent use. If the consultants are constantly developing their skills, they can continue to make innovative contributions. Furthermore, they can serve as a link with outside resources such as universities and research programs, and more importantly, they can serve to help keep the OD effort at the highest possible professional and ethical level. Their skills and insights should serve as a standard against which to compare the activities of internal change agents.

Another dimension of the issue arises, however, when the consultant senses that his assistance is no longer needed—perhaps when there is too much effort made to keep him busy. For the client's good, to avoid wasting his own professional resources, and to be congruent, the consultant should confront the issue.

CONCLUDING COMMENTS

Explicit in the above is the need for the consultants and the consultant teams to model effective interpersonal and group behavior in their relationships with the client system, not only to enhance their direct impact but to facilitate their role as educators and as those whose skills are worth emulating. In short, consulting behavior will tend to reinforce or disconfirm learning that occurs.

[9] Chris Argyris, *Intervention Theory and Method: A Behavioral Science View* (Reading, Mass.: Addison-Wesley Publishing Company, 1970), pp. 16–19. This quotation, p. 18.

One of the most helpful ways to bring this about is to have consultant–key client teams and consulting teams manage the culture of their own teams consciously and collaboratively. Thus, the key parties in the OD effort not only are modeling the most effective behavior they know when they are in contact with the broader client system but also are helping each other with the growth and development of their own temporary units and in terms of their own personal growth and development. This is not to suggest that perfection is demanded of consultant behavior or consultant–key client behavior—this expectation would be paralyzing—but we are suggesting that adequate attention to the culture of the OD process itself can pay large dividends.

At a broader level, action research needs to be utilized relative to the entire OD process. This requires the establishment of appropriate feedback loops relative to the various components and phases of the process. This presents still an additional challenge to the consultant-client relationship—both parties will need to collaborate if an effective monitoring of the OD effort is to take place.

17

Mechanistic and Organic Systems and the Contingency Approach

Two types of organizations, *mechanistic* and *organic,* have been described by Tom Burns and G. M. Stalker; in this chapter we wish to explore the relevance of these concepts to organization development. These terms are being used with increasing frequency, and it is important to understand their meanings and the implications of one system versus the other. These terms can be useful shorthand ways of describing the overall "climate" or mode of operating in an organization or its subunits, but, unfortunately, they can also be used as "bad" or "good" labels. *Mechanistic,* in particular, is frequently used with a "bad" connotation. In general, OD activities tend to result in an organization beginning to take on more *organic* characteristics, but some paradoxes and contingencies need examining.

According to Burns and Stalker, these two types of organizations, mechanistic and organic, in their pure form, are seen as located on opposite ends of a continuum and not as a dichotomy.[1] Various organizations will be found at different points between these polarities and indeed may move back and forth along this continuum, depending upon the degree of stability or change being experienced. In addition, an organization may include both types within its subdivisions.

> Both types represent a "rational" form of organization, in that they may both, in our experience, be explicitly and deliberately created and maintained to exploit the human resources of a concern in the most efficient manner feasible in the circumstances of the concern. Not surprisingly, however, each exhibits characteristics which have been hitherto associated with different kinds of interpretation. For it is our contention that empirical findings have usually been classified according to sociological

[1] Tom Burns and G. M. Stalker, *The Management of Innovation* (London: Tavistock Publications, 1961), pp. 119–25.

ideology rather than according to the functional specificity of the working organization to its task and the conditions confronting it.[2]

Thus, implicitly, Burns and Stalker do not see the occurrence of one or the other of these two systems as necessarily accidental, but as frequently stemming from the circumstances being faced by the organization. It would also seem to be implicit that the occurrence of one or the other might also stem from an ideological preference—a phenomenon that could represent a trap for overzealous adherents to either type of organization.

MECHANISTIC SYSTEMS

To elaborate on the two types, Burns and Stalker see the *mechanistic* form of organization as particularly appropriate to stable conditions and having the following characteristics:

1. A high degree of task differentiation and specialization, precise delineation of rights and responsibilities and methods to be used, and role incumbents tending to pursue technical improvements in means in contrast to focusing on the overall ends of the organization.
2. A high degree of reliance on each hierarchical level for task coordination, control, and communications. That is, each supervisor is responsible for reconciling the activities below him.
3. A tendency for the top of the hierarchy to control incoming and outgoing communications and to be conservative in dispensing information within the system. (Burns and Stalker give an example of a manager who literally controlled *all* correspondence in and out of the firm.)
4. A high degree of emphasis on vertical interactions between superiors and subordinates, with subordinate activities mainly governed by these interactions. (While Burns and Stalker do not say this, clearly there is an informal social system involving lateral peer interactions which stays mainly "underground" under these circumstances.)
5. Insistence on loyalty to the organization and to superiors.
6. A higher value placed on internal (local) knowledge, skill, and experience, in contrast to more general (cosmopolitan) knowledge, skill, and experience.[3]

[2] *Ibid.*, p. 119.

[3] *Ibid.*, pp. 119–20. In some respects the mechanistic form of organization is comparable to the "bureaucratic" organization as described by Weber. For example, the features of the bureaucratic form, to Weber, include a "clearly defined hierarchy of offices," emphasis on impersonal rules, and administrators "subject to strict and systematic discipline and control." Max Weber, *The Theory of Social and Economic Organization* (New York: Oxford University Press, Inc., 1957), pp. 333–34. See also William G. Scott, *Organization Theory: A Behavioral Analysis for Management* (Homewood, Ill.: Richard D. Irwin, Inc., 1967), Chap. 12.

Another characteristic, which is not explicit but is perhaps implied in Burns and Stalker's model and which we believe to be one of the key characteristics of a mechanistic system, is:

7. A one-to-one leadership style, that is, with most interactions between superior and subordinate occurring in private discussion, and an absence or minimal attention to group processes and the informal system. As seen in this form of organization, the superior-subordinate relationship tends to be a telling-reporting relationship. (See Figure 17-1.) To illustrate the existence of such a leadership style, we have had managers tell us that, literally, their superior had never held a meeting involving all his immediate subordinates. They also said that most of the one-to-one conversations centered around assignments initiated by the superior, and in his office, i.e., on his "turf."

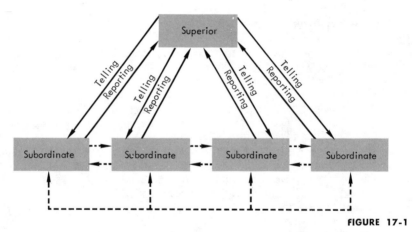

FIGURE 17-1

CHARACTERISTIC PATTERN OF LEADERSHIP
IN A MECHANISTIC SYSTEM

ORGANIC SYSTEMS

In contrast, the *organic* system is seen by Burns and Stalker as appropriate to changing conditions and has the following characteristics.[4]

1. A continuous reassessment of tasks and assignments through interaction with others and a high value placed on utilizing special knowledge and

[4] Burns and Stalker, *The Management of Innovation*, pp. 119–25. Bennis uses the term *organic-adaptive* in describing a similar type of organization. See Warren Bennis, "Organizations of the Future," *Personnel Administration*, 30 (September–October 1967), 6–19.

experience which can contribute to the "real" problems being faced by the organization.

2. A network of authority, control, and communication, stemming more from expertise and commitment to the total task than from the omniscience of the chief executive or the authority of hierarchical roles. Centers of control and communication are frequently *ad hoc*, that is, are located where the knowledge is. Responsibility is viewed as something to be shared rather than narrowly delimited.

Although the organic systems "remain stratified," they tend to be stratified more on the basis of expertise:

> The lead in joint decisions is frequently taken by seniors, but it is an essential presumption of the organic system that the lead, i.e., "authority," is taken by whoever shows himself most informed and capable, i.e., the "best authority." The location of authority is settled by consensus.[5]

3. A tendency for communications to be much more extensive and open in contrast to limited and controlled. (This is more implicit in Burns and Stalker's model than explicit.)

4. The encouragement of a communications pattern and style which is lateral and diagonal as well as vertical and which is more of a consultative, information- and advice-giving nature than of a command or decision-relying nature. By *diagonal* we refer to Burns and Stalker's notion about communications between people of different rank and across functional groups.

5. A greater emphasis on commitment to the organization's tasks, progress, and growth than on obedience or loyalty.

6. High value placed on expertise relevant to the technological and commercial milieu of the organization (cosmopolitan skills). One indicator would be "importance and prestige attach[ed] to affiliations...."[6]

And finally, to supplement this model, a characteristic that we believe to be central to a truly organic system:

7. A team leadership style, with an emphasis on consultation and considerable attention to interpersonal and group processes, including methods of decision making and more frequent decision by consensus.[7] (See Figure 17-2.) Perhaps symbolically, meetings are frequently held away from the superior's office, with physical facilities designed to further group dialogue.

[5] *Ibid.*, p. 122.

[6] *Ibid.*, p. 121.

[7] Likert contrasts *man-man* and *group* patterns of organization which are comparable to the two types of leadership styles we are contrasting. See Rensis Likert, *New Patterns of Leadership* (New York: McGraw-Hill Book Company, 1961), pp. 106–10.

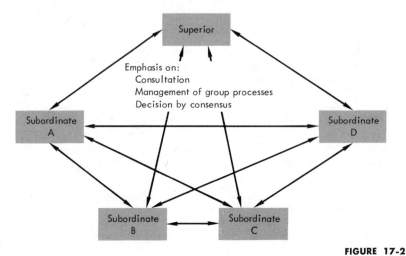

FIGURE 17-2

CHARACTERISTIC PATTERN OF LEADERSHIP
IN AN ORGANIC SYSTEM

THE CONTINGENCY QUESTION

From our experience, organization development activities tend to shift an organization toward the organic mode as described by the above seven characteristics. The reason, of course, is that there is a deliberate emphasis in an OD program toward collaboratively managed group culture and collaboratively managed organizational culture. Whether we call it collaboration, consultation, or open communications, the theme in OD is effective participation. And that theme pervades most of the characteristics of an organic system.

Paradoxically, however, while the thrust of an organization development effort is toward the organic mode, OD activities sometimes increase the mechanistic quality of some organizational dimensions. For example, consensus might develop in a work team so that it would be functional for duties and responsibilities to be more precisely defined or so that there should be more reliance on the superior for coordination and control in the assignment of routine tasks. At the level of examining its methods, the team has organic characteristics; at the level of routine tasks, the team is deciding to become more mechanistic. As another illustration, an organization development effort might strengthen the organic characteristics of the design and engineering departments of an automobile company, while the assembly line departments might remain substantially mechanistic in terms of task delineation although becoming more organic in terms of employee involvement in the control function.

Thus, it will not suffice to have an ideological adherence to one form of organization over the other. There are unquestionably contingencies that affect the appropriateness of one system over the other or the appropriateness of a particular mix of characteristics of the two systems.

We have already noted that Burns and Stalker see the mechanistic form of organization as appropriate to "stable conditions" and the organic form to "changing conditions." Joan Woodward in a study in South Essex, England, found that successful manufacturing firms of the "large-batch production" type (assembly line, or large-batch production) tended to be mechanistic, while successful firms of the unit and "small-batch" (e.g., prototype production) and "process production" (e.g., continuous flow liquids production) tended to be organic.[8] Another study, by Lawrence and Lorsch, found that production units within six firms had a much more formalized structure than the research laboratories in the same firms.[9]

Morse and Lorsch in a study of two research laboratories with unpredictable research and development tasks—one an "effective performer" and one "less effective"—and two container plants involving the manufacture of standarized items with automated, high-speed production lines —again, one plant effective and one less effective—found that the more-effective units had a better "fit" between structure and organizational climate than the less-effective units. The high-performing lab featured scientists' perceptions of minimal and flexible rules, a long-term approach to reviews and reporting, minimal control on their behavior, and high influence on their part. In contrast, the less-effective lab was more restrictive and restraining, more rule oriented, and more structured, with more decisions made at the top.

At the rank-and-file level of the more-effective manufacturing plant, there were comprehensive rules, procedures, and control systems and short-range reporting and review sessions, and there was relatively low rank-and-file influence with a corresponding directive-type supervisor. Thus, influence tended to be concentrated at higher levels. Conversely, in the less-effective container plant, practices were less controlling and structured, with a more participative kind of supervision. In both the

---

[8] Joan Woodward, *Industrial Organization: Theory and Practice* (London: Oxford University Press, 1965), p. 71. A rationale that we see for process organizations to be organic is that the equipment does most of the routine work while employees are largely busy with planning, research, and monitoring functions.

[9] Paul R. Lawrence and Jay Lorsch, *Organization and Environment: Managing Differentiation and Integration* (Boston: Graduate School of Business Administration, Harvard University, 1967), p. 32.

effective research lab and the effective plant, employees expressed more feelings of competence than did their counterparts in the less-effective organizations; the researchers concluded that the more effective fit between task, structure, and climate resulted in more feelings of competence, and implicitly, organizational effectiveness.[10] (For a summary of the study, see Table 17-1.) While Morse and Lorsch acknowledge the difficulty in imputing cause-and-effect relationships—for example, do feelings of competence stem from unit effectiveness or from the fit between these various dimensions? [11]—the point is that a number of contingencies may determine the "best" structure, "best" design of tasks, or "best" leadership style, and so forth.[12]

In short, the contingency approach suggests that the question is not "Which is better, an organic system or a mechanistic system?" but that the question needs to be posed in terms of contingencies. For example:

1. What is the most effective mix of organic and mechanistic characteristics for a given organization or unit and its current circumstances? Or,
2. Under what conditions is the organic system superior to the mechanistic, and vice versa? Or,
3. Given different technologies, tasks, and human resources, what dimensions do we expect to change with OD-type interventions? Or,
4. Under what circumstances is an organization development effort particularly relevant or most likely to succeed?

While we intend to be somewhat specific in answering the latter question in the final chapter, the following are some of the contingencies that we see as the most relevant in answering question 2—Under what conditions is the organic system superior to the mechanistic, and vice-versa?

Contingency of:

a. Hierarchical level—the more extensive the role requirements in terms of planning, coordination, control, and decision making. The higher the level and thus the more complexity in these functions, the more the need for extensive inputs from diverse specialists and for examining many

---

[10] John J. Morse and Jay W. Lorsch, "Beyond Theory Y," *Harvard Business Review,* 48 (May–June 1970), 61–68.

[11] *Ibid.,* p. 66.

[12] Robert Tannenbaum and Warren Schmidt describe a number of contingencies in leadership in their well known essay, "How to Choose a Leadership Pattern," *Harvard Business Review,* 36 (March–April 1958), 95–101. Fred Fiedler has done extensive research relative to what he calls a "Contingency Model of Leadership Effectiveness." See Fred E. Fiedler, *A Theory of Leadership Effectiveness* (New York: McGraw-Hill Book Company, 1967).

TABLE 17-1

SYSTEM CONTINGENCIES IN FOUR ORGANIZATIONS

Type of Organization	Tasks	Structure	Climate	Feelings of Competence	Organizational Effectiveness
Manufacturing plant	Predictable manufacturing tasks	Highly structured and defined roles, duties, relationships	Influence concentrated at the top	Higher	Effective
Manufacturing plant		Less structured and defined	Egalitarian distribution of influence	Lower	Less effective
Research laboratory	Uncertain research tasks	Low degree of structure in roles, duties, and relationships	Egalitarian distribution of influence	Higher	Effective
Research laboratory		More structure	Influence tending to concentrate at the top	Lower	Less effective

Based on our interpretation of material in John J. Morse and Jay W. Lorsch, "Beyond Theory Y," *Harvard Business Review*, 48 (May–June 1970), 61–68.

options; thus the need for acknowledging expertise, for open communications, for clarifying goals, and so forth.

b. Interdependency—the more that role performance is directly associated with the discretionary actions of others. (This contingency is related to the previous one.) The more interdependency, the more that communications need to be open, the more team leadership style is appropriate, and so forth.

c. Skills—the capabilities and talents of the human resources in the system. The greater the cognitive, problem-solving, and interpersonal capabilities of the people in the system, the more the organic style will work. The organic system is more demanding of people at all levels than is the mechanistic form of organizations.

d. Group process skills—the more effectively that the leader and the subordinates have basic communications, task, and maintenance skills. In particular, skills in group processes are a necessary prerequisite to a team leadership style; such skills are also important in the effective functioning of taskforces, committees, and so forth.

e. Rapidity of external change. The more the organization is existing in a rapidly changing environment, the more important the adaptability facilitated by the organic mode. Burns and Stalker see this dimension as particularly important.

f. Time pressure, danger, or external threat. For example, although the organic system may be better prepared to cope with future uncertainty, at the time of an unanticipated crisis the organization may need to revert to highly mechanistic characteristics to survive.

g. Technology—the degree to which tasks are predetermined by the machinery or methods of a particular industry. For example, the technology of an assembly line serves to preplan tasks, to narrow interdependency, and so forth.

h. Attitudes or assumptions about people in organizations—a "Theory X" versus a "Theory Y" set of assumptions. A Theory X set of assumptions will tend to be incompatible with the culture of an organic system. In contrast, if key executives or subordinates are philosophically committed to a participative or democratic leadership style, such values will tend to be more congruent with the organic style than with the mechanistic.

SUMMARY AND CONCLUSION

Mechanistic and *organic* organizations have been contrasted to provide rubrics for thinking about the outcomes of organization development activities. While, in general, OD strategies tend to increase the organic characteristics of a system, paradoxically they can also lead to an increase in mechanistic attributes along certain dimensions, for example, an increase in task differentiation at lower levels of the organization, or more stringent procedures.

Theory and some research suggest that neither the purely organic form nor the purely mechanistic form may be optimal under all circumstances but that there needs to be a good "fit" between technology, tasks, organization climate, and human resources. Thus, different organization development interventions may have differing degrees of relevance under different circumstances. And those circumstances may vary by hierarchical levels, interdependency, skills and group process skills, time pressure and rapidity of external change, danger or external threat, technology, and values.

The genius of OD, however, is that the perceptions, feelings, and cognitive inputs of organizational members are tapped to build an optimal, evolving, organizational design for the unique circumstances faced by the organization and its members. Thus the thrust of OD activities is to be responsive to the data—not to impose an organic system. In the process, however, the organization is likely to become more organic.

18

The Future of OD

Organizational development represents one of today's leading edges of applied behavioral science as organization theorists and practitioners endeavor to find ways to improve organizational effectiveness and achieve organizational excellence. OD appears to be co-opting a sizable portion of the behavioral science and practitioner talent; [1] it seems to be absorbing increasing amounts of internal resources of organizational time and manpower; there is prolific growth of practitioners and concomitant professional groups; increasingly OD seems to be chosen over such other organizational change techniques as sensitivity training, management by objectives, job enrichment, and management development seminars—at least over these techniques as isolated "packages"; in sum, it looks as though OD's time has come. In this chapter we look at organization development—a social invention and a change technique—from the point of view of its permanence as a form of applied behavioral science. We believe that some of the foundations of OD and some of its practices augur well for its continued value and validity in improving organizations.

Fad is defined as "a fashion in dress, behavior, or speech that enjoys

[1] It is interesting to note that of the eight behavioral scientists who are mentioned most frequently by industrial executives as having been of influence to them personally, the late Douglas McGregor, Frederick Herzberg, Rensis Likert, Chris Argyris, the late Abraham Maslow, Robert Blake and/or Jane Mouton, and Warren Bennis—in that order—at least six have been directly involved in organization development activities. McGregor, Likert, Argyris, Blake and Mouton, and Bennis have all been organization development consultants and have written or lectured extensively on the subject. See Harold M. F. Rush, *Behavioral Science Concepts and Management Application* (New York: National Industrial Conference Board, Studies in Personnel Policy, No. 216, 1969), pp. 9–10.

brief popularity." [2] Clearly OD is being embraced enthusiastically by many applied behavioral scientists, organization theorists, and organizations. The critical issues, then, have to do with whether it will last on the social science practice scene and also whether it has substance and a fundamental quality. Let us examine some of the strengths and the weaknesses of organization development. Following that we will express our opinion in answering the question, Is OD a passing fad?

SOME OF THE STRENGTHS OF OD

Organization development draws upon a large number of models, theories, and practices; it borrows freely from the proven procedures for improving the functioning of individuals, groups, and organizations. OD is an amalgam, a culmination from diverse sources, and as such represents the resultant of the best thinking from the behavioral sciences. The foundations and characteristics of OD discussed in Chapter 5 suggest to us that OD is made of solid stuff. The action research model, a systems approach to understanding organizational dynamics, and a change strategy that focuses on the culture of work teams and the organization—all these features of organization development serve to make it more powerful and relevant than most change strategies of the past. In addition, a systematic, planned approach utilizing an overall improvement strategy assures that the desirable features of OD are capitalized upon.

The action research model, for example, is a model for *tracking*—for staying on target, for discarding alternatives that do not meet the test of efficacy in the real world. Not only is it a good model for improvement of an organization (with its emphasis on goal setting, data collecting, and action planning by the organization members themselves), it is also a good model for keeping the practice of OD flexible, responsive to changing demands, and open to new ideas and practices. In effect, we are suggesting that application of the action research paradigm to the practice of OD will keep it from becoming irrelevant to the needs of individuals and organizations.

The focus on organization culture is another strong feature of OD that portends future success. Individual beliefs, values, attitudes, and behaviors are so overwhelmingly determined by, and are a part of, organization culture that change efforts directed toward other facets of the individual, such as personality, physical environment, and the like,

---

[2] *The American Heritage Dictionary of the English Language* (Boston: American Heritage Publishing Company and Houghton Mifflin Company, 1969), p. 470.

will probably have only minimal impact, while change efforts directed toward culture will have significant impact. But OD as a process does not just recognize the importance of culture—it also suggests ways of analyzing culture and changing culture. These are the real steps of progress. Mastery over one's culture rather than subjugation to it is a profound thought. OD represents some definite steps in this direction and thus distinguishes itself from other change efforts.

There seems to be historical evidence that permanent change in individuals and groups is facilitated by working with the intact group rather than with isolated individuals. This finding is no doubt related to the importance of culture in determining behaviors. For example, in part, the laboratory-training movement attempted to improve organizational functioning by having key individuals attend sensitivity-training labs. This practice had only limited payoff in terms of organizational change. On the other hand, working with real, intact work groups has been found to have tremendous potency for increasing effectiveness of individuals and groups. Since a central tenet of OD is that of working with the teams of the organization, OD appears to be on a quite solid base in this regard.

While organization development facilitates change in individuals and organizations, there is a genuine sense in which OD also brings stability. OD represents an application of the scientific method of problem solving to human, social, and organizational problems. There is great solidity and stability in having such a model to base solutions upon. Change occurs, of course, when people are moved from a traditional, or haphazard, problem-solving modality to that of the scientific method. But stability occurs when individuals, groups, and organizations learn to apply this method to all sorts of events in the organization. Change occurs, of course, when the win-lose, boundary-defending, competitive relations between groups are altered by organization development efforts aimed at improving intergroup relations and intergroup effectiveness. But stability occurs when the awareness of interdependence of goals and efforts and the benefits of cooperation lead to reward for the groups. We believe that the benefits of OD are stability as well as managed changes. If this is so, OD has a much stronger chance of survival.

SOME CONTINGENCIES

We see a number of contingencies in the future viability of OD. Probably the most serious handicap of OD as it has emerged historically is its overpreoccupation with the human and social dynamics of organizations to the detriment of attending to the task, technical, and structural aspects and their interdependencies. This statement reflects an imbalance of effort and perhaps a lack of skills on the part of the practitioners, not a total disregard for these other areas. Bennis wrote to this point in an editorial in the *Journal of Applied Behavioral Sciences* as follows:

> I have yet to see an organization development program that uses an interventional strategy other than an interpersonal one, and this is serious when one considers that the most pivotal strategies of change in our society are political, legal and technological. We call ourselves "change agents," but the real changes in our society have been wrought by the pill, the bomb, the automobile, industrialization, communication media, and other forces of modernization.[3]

While we have seen a number of OD efforts that have featured minimum interventions at the interpersonal level and maximum attention to goal setting and structural changes, Bennis's point is well taken.

In the future, organization development specialists must know much more about such matters and must establish linkages with practitioners in such fields as management science, personnel and industrial psychology, operations research, and industrial engineering in order to provide a broader range of options for organizational intervention. Such broader knowledge, when integrated with OD techniques, will be particularly relevant in the second or subsequent phases of OD efforts, that is, probably after the first cycle of diagnosis, data feedback, problem discussion, and action planning. For example, the job description exercise in Illustration 4 of Chapter 1 is a marriage of OD and personnel management techniques and was used in the second phase of an OD effort.

In addition to OD practitioners knowing more about personnel management, industrial engineering, and the like, specialists in other fields will undoubtedly be learning much more about OD in the future. The result should be enhanced cooperation between the OD specialists as well as staff interventions that are much more congruent and complementary with the cultures emerging from OD efforts. A danger, of course, is that less-than-qualified people will zealously apply OD techniques out of joint with other events. A rash of such occurrences in a number of organizations could seriously jeopardize the long-range viability of OD.

In a recent speech Burke voiced some other worries about OD. "OD has a future if it can act in the present to avoid premature formulation, develop strategies for coping with immediate crises and for sustaining long-term efforts, avoid being co-opted by traditional organizational

---

[3] Cited in W. G. Bennis, *Organization Development: Its Nature, Origins and Prospects* (Reading, Mass.: Addison-Wesley Publishing Company, 1969), pp. 78–79.

pressures, and continue to develop and refine a value system that will be required for organizational viability and renewal." [4] These issues identified by Burke appear to be both things to avoid and goals to be accomplished for OD. In this same speech, Burke predicts that OD will increasingly become more interdisciplinary, calling on operations research specialists and others.

Another significant contingency lies in the conceptual foundation underlying OD strategies. OD is limited to the models of planned change that it utilizes. OD represents the state-of-the-art, but the current state is that we have a rather limited number of models for effecting permanent change. For example, OD seems restricted in its models regarding effective use of power in organizations. Stemming from the laboratory training method background, models of change underlying OD interventions typically involve love-trust, collaborative models rather than those involving power, coercion, or competition.[5] We have no quarrel with the collaborative model but rather are appealing for the development of additional, perhaps contingency, models. All the models will still have to be tested in the crucible of ongoing organizations. It may be that with the development of new and different models that come to grips with the issue of power in organizations or that treat power in different ways, OD as practiced today will require modification. It seems to us that contributions such as Walton's in the area of third-party peacemaking increase the range of models available for more effective management of power issues in OD efforts.[6]

Another possible handicap to the viability of OD is that it represents a long-term and expensive investment on the part of client organizations. OD technology has developed to the state that client systems and consultants working together can in fact bring about organization improvement when there is enough time—when there is a long-range change project. OD does not have quick remedies; OD does not offer shortcuts to total organization improvement. Significant organization improvement requires that there be a stabilization of the complicated fabric of organization culture at successively more effective levels—this takes time and much effort on the part of organizational members.

Another major contingency in the future viability of OD lies in the degree of congruence between the emerging internal organizational culture resulting from OD efforts and the cultures of the organization's

[4] W. W. Burke, "Organization Development: Here to Stay?" A paper presented to the annual convention of the Academy of Management, August 17, 1971, Atlanta, Georgia, p. 13.

[5] For an elaboration of this point, see Bennis, *Organization Development,* pp. 77–79.

[6] See R. E. Walton, *Interpersonal Peacemaking, Confrontations and Third Party Consultation* (Reading, Mass.: Addison-Wesley Publishing Company, 1969).

various external interfaces. Our hypothesis is as follows: the higher the congruence, the greater the potential viability of the OD effort. As an illustration, if the internal culture of a manufacturing company professes honesty, but if that part of the interface between company and consumer under the control of the company has elements of deception, the internal environment will ultimately take on some of the same quality. As another example, if resource development is the internal slogan but resource exploitation is the external practice, a spreading internal cynicism among organizational members can be predicted. One can, however, also be optimistic about such incongruities. A long-range OD effort is likely to result in people confronting such issues and greatly improving the quality of the external interfaces.

OD AND THE EXTERNAL ENVIRONMENT

To elaborate on the relationship between OD and the external environment there are a number of likely occurrences that we believe will have an impact on the interest shown in OD. The rapid awakening to the grave dangers of environmental pollution and exploitation is likely to provide impetus to an examination of the quality of life in organizations. We believe that people are increasingly going to be concerned with the quality of organizational life, particularly in those organizations where people earn their livelihood. For example, more and more we are going to realize the important linkages between mental health on the one hand and leadership style and group processes on the other, and the similar linkages between physical health, motivation, and the meaning of one's work. People are increasingly going to be intolerant of organizational cultures that treat human resources as relative passive entities mainly to be selected, directed, and evaluated. People want much more control over their destinies than that, and their impatience with such cultures will become more and more evident. Such concerns for the quality of life in both the physical and the organizational environment will provide, we believe, an acceleration of interest in organization development.

Reciprocally, it should be recognized that internal OD activities will have important effects in the community. For example, the marketing manager who has developed real skill in group methods is likely to become highly influential in such matters as meeting improvement, problem diagnosis, and climate setting when he finds himself on a church board or on the executive committee of a civic organization. The director of nursing who has had a long-range collaborative involvement in a hospital OD effort is likely to be an extraordinarily effective facilitator in her professional association or her club. The machinist who is familiar with attitude surveys and problem-solving meetings may become a catalyst around whom union meetings become more participative, more problem-solving oriented.

WILL OD BE A PASSING FAD?

We have three points to make relative to whether or not OD will be a passing fad. First, we are convinced that OD will be around and will survive for many years to come; second, current OD technology will undoubtedly be superseded by additional or modified practices as the years unfold; and third, there will always be a need for something like OD. OD is partially a response to the needs of both individuals and organizations for improvement strategies that will bring individual aspirations and organizational objectives together. There will always be that need.

We do not believe OD is a passing fad. OD will evolve new forms, new technologies, new concepts, and new models in the future as it changes and grows with new inputs from practitioners and clients in many different situations. It will continue to reflect the state-of-the-art even as that art changes. OD will probably be enlarged in scope in the future, encompassing specialists from such disciplines as organization theory, operations research, personnel and industrial relations, community development, and mental health. Through the 1970s OD will be on the increase; it will become more widely used by different kinds of organizations. Long-term relationships may permit and encourage more evaluation research on OD, and in addition, the causal dynamics of interventions may increasingly come under scrutiny.

Beckhard suggests that the theme of the seventies is the "active and continuing search for organization excellence." [7] OD is the only comprehensive technology we see at the present time that will enable that goal to be reached. Thousands of managers worldwide will be engaged in that search. To many, OD will almost intuitively be perceived as congruent with the intentions they have been attempting to carry out in their organizations—intentions that have heretofore been handicapped by the lack of such a comprehensive improvement technology.

Blake and Mouton likewise voice "optimism" for the future of OD.[8]

[7] Richard Beckhard, *Organization Development: Strategies and Models* (Reading, Mass.: Addison-Wesley Publishing Company, 1969), p. 116. Italics deleted.
[8] R. R. Blake and J. S. Mouton, "OD—Fad or Fundamental," *Training and Development Journal*, 24 (January 1970), 9–16.

Their argument is that OD is based on behavioral science in a fundamental way and that this foundation will contribute to its continued viability. Bennis also foresees a good future for OD. He says, "... basically, organization development is one of the few educational programs I know of that has the potential to create an institution vital enough to cope with the unparalleled changes ahead." [9]

We agree with these assessments.

CONCLUDING COMMENTS

Historically, organization development has largely emerged from two interrelated origins: (*a*) innovations stemming from difficulties encountered in utilizing laboratory training in the solution of work team and larger system problems and (*b*) innovations centering around the effective feedback of attitude survey data. The action research model is common to both.

Organization development is based on a set of assumptions and values about people and groups in organizations, about the nature of total systems, and about the nature of the client-consultant relationship, and it has a substantial base in behavioral science research and theory. Intervention strategies of the behavioral scientist–change agent tend to be based on an action research model and tend to be focused more on helping the people in an organization learn to solve problems rather than on prescribing how things should be done differently.

Successful organization development efforts require skillful interventions, a systems view, top management support and involvement, an open and shared technology and value system, and a long-rage perspective. In addition, to be sustained, changes stemming from organization development must be linked to changes in such organization subsystems as the appraisal, reward, staffing, bargaining, and leadership subsystems.

The future viability of organization development efforts has many dimensions, including the degree to which the OD efforts accurately reflect the perceptions, concerns, and aspirations of the participating members. Other dimensions include the degree to which OD practitioners are innovative and successful in helping bring about congruence with other programs aimed at organization improvement, such as job enrichment, work simplification, and management by objectives; the degree to which theorists and practitioners develop additional conceptual models;

[9] Bennis, *Organization Development,* p. 82.

and the quality and extent of research on the effectiveness of various intervention strategies.

Successful organization development tends to be a total system effort, a process of planned improvement—not a program with a temporary quality; it is aimed at developing the organization's internal resources for effective change in the future. Its real thrusts are for organizational members to draw out and help develop the resources of each other and to increase the range of behavioral options open to individuals and teams. Furthermore, it is a collaborative process of managing the culture of the organization—not something that is done *to* somebody, but a transactional process of people working together to improve their mutual effectiveness in attaining their mutual objectives.

Index

DATE DUE

APR - 6 1999		
ILL (DEL)		
1646042		
02/13/05		
ILL (PAS)		
1824600		
04/23/06		

DEMCO 13829810